D1430310

HELENE HANFF:
A LIFE

Grand Oak Books

ISBN 9780982957936

ISBN 0-9829579-3-9

Library of Congress Cataloging-in-Publication Data:

Pastore, Stephen R./Helene Hanff: A Life

Hanff, Helene (1916-1994)
                    p.   cm.

First Edition

Helene Hanff:
A Life

by

Stephen R. Pastore

Grand Oak Books
New York

Genealogy of Helene Marjorie Hanff

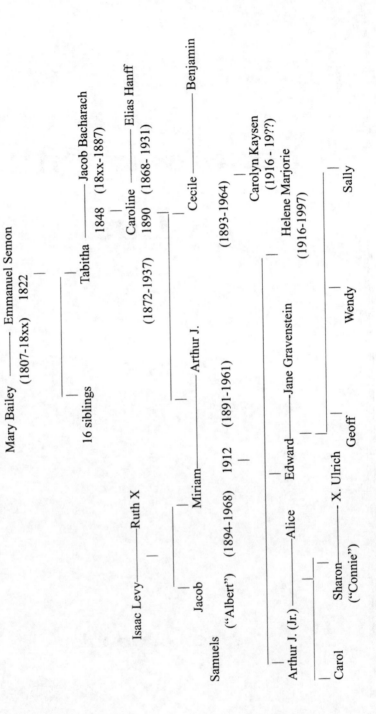

PROLOGUE

"Sleep has never been a problem. I need seven hours and if I'm in bed by midnight, I beat the alarm clock by 15 minutes. A beep is no way to wake anyone up.

It's a big production between stepping out of bed at 7am and sitting down to breakfast an hour later. Day-beds and furniture that folds up into the walls are for people whose kids come home occasionally, or for putting up visitors short-term. I've had enough of them. What you're sitting on is my beautifully sprung bed. However, there's a price to pay for having my room the way I want it. Each morning, I remove the pillows, fold the sheets and blankets into neat piles and hide them all in a cupboard.

My bed routine is followed by the search for contact lenses, and washing and dressing. When I finally get to sit down with a glass of orange juice, eggs, bacon, coffee and toast spread with the finest no- sugar marmalade in the world—believe me—breakfast is a triumph!

I'm a diabetic. For years I had low blood sugar and steered clear- of sugar to prevent diabetes. I got it anyway. Here's some advice for your skinny, diabetic senior citizen readers: *stay off sugar*. Although thee official line is no sugar, I'm so thin my doctor said sugar was OK for me. I ignored him because I was sure it caused leg cramps. When my brother recommended a pudding he'd discovered which was sugar-free, I indulged myself; and sure enough, that night I woke up with excruciating leg cramps. The pain was so bad I thought I'd wake the entire building. I checked the ingredients on the box. The first one was 'corn dextrose'—another way of saying sugar. Was I furious!

Over breakfast, I listen to public radio and classical music and read the Sunday edition of *The New York Times*. Anyone who tells you they read it on Sunday is lying. There are not enough hours in the day. Have you seen the size of it? Last year, two weeks before Christmas, my neighbor asked me to bring a copy home for her. In the store, I took one look at it and went home for my shopping cart. Besides thee magazine, books, news, entertainment, real estate and financial supplements, there was a ton of special advertising. A person could slip a disc carrying one paper, never mind two.

At 9am I do the dishes and then get down to whatever work there is. I need to be busy. Now I'm updating my walking guide to New York—*Apple of My Eye*. It's for visitors to the city, suggesting places I think have something special to offer. I wrote the original book 12 years ago -with my friend Patsy. She lived on the West Side and we had a marvelous time meeting once a week for 13 weeks, going out on field trips. Patsy was in her forties, married, with a family, and died of cancer. Now I've lost four friends who were 20 years younger than me, which is spooky. I haven't enjoyed many of the field trips this time round because many places remind me of all the good times I had with Patsy.

So much has changed in New York since I wrote *Apple of My Eye*. Some buildings weren't even a footnote, so wherever necessary I'm adding 'PS—12 years later'. One of the most exciting places is Battery Park City, Lower Manhattan. It's the business centre near City Hall. No one lived there 12 years ago. They commuted to work and the place emptied at 5:30 pm. Now it's a thriving new community, jumping 24 hours a day and I love it. I don't love the latest building of the Metropolitan Museum which has eaten into even more acres of Central Park and makes me blind with rage.

I adore Central Park, especially with the changing seasons. It's vast and not a space you can lock like places in London and Paris. New York isn't any less safe than other big cities, but you need some common sense. I wouldn't recommend walking around a London slum at night any more than I would advise it in New York. Some British theatre nuts I know—The Derek Jacobi Cadets—came to see him in New York. Rather than spend money on a hotel, they camped down on Broadway so they could see him on stage twice. They told me they felt safer there at night than they would have done on Charing Cross Road.

If my neighbor hears the typewriter she doesn't come in for morning coffee, but was I glad she came today. She rescued me from The Index, which is hard work—all those cross references and alphabetical orders. I use a manual typewriter on the grounds that it won't matter if there's a power cut and I have a deadline to meet. The real reason I don't like electric typewriters is the noise. If my 1964 model breaks down before I do, I guess I'll replace it, but it looks as though we'll both go at roughly the same time.

You needn't cook in New York, unless, like me, you have to be careful about food. Once in a while I buy pizza, which isn't really substantial if I'm going walking. By 3pm I'm just about ready to climb up the walls of this apartment and I try to walk 40 or 50 blocks a day for the exercise. I need a destination—Saks or the library. I still haunt libraries because there are plenty of books I want to read, but I don't necessarily want to own them. Books I love most are diaries and memories. I'm trying a short story by the English novelist Elizabeth Taylor to see, once more, if I'll like fiction. We all know I won't.

Sometimes I meet visitors at the St Regis—where, because of the diabetes, I can't even enjoy a martini—or at Rumpelmayers for tea, where I daren't touch the gorgeous pastries. If it wasn't for the rain and the thought of having to wait ages for a bus, I'd have met you there. I didn't want you to see my curtains, which need washing. I'm waiting for tall neighbors to take them down for me. They're away and I'm looking after their pot plants. It's a friendly block, I even know all the dogs, and Emily, a sweet little toddler from next door, comes to me for a change of scenery.

Since I had pneumonia, which is when the doctors discovered the diabetes, I've had to restrict how many cigarettes I smoke each day. Usually it's nine, but if I'm under stress it goes up to 10. After that, I start wheezing and coughing which is horrible. Before I go to sleep, having taken the pillows, the sheets and the blankets from their hiding place, made my bed, spent half an hour cleaning my contact lenses and changing to my cataract glasses, I reckon I deserve five minutes of my final cigarette

Inscribed to Helene by Ms. Bancroft

INTRODUCTION

I moved back to New York City from Miami Beach in 1986. By 1987 I lived in a pre-war building on Third Avenue between 47th and 48th Streets on Manhattan's East Side. As it turned out I was only twenty some-odd blocks from Helene Hanff's apartment on East 72nd Street. Within a few months, I had started a correspondence with her and in less than a year I was visiting her 8th floor apartment two or three times a week. Initially we spoke about New York City and how I had grown quite tired of what I called the daily humiliations: waiting on lines for bad movies, having my car abused by foreign and gruff parking attendants, and the high price of groceries, telephone service and electricity. One December I brought her the Christmas cards I received from my building's staff, numbering thirty one; everyone from trash collectors to elevator repairmen, to assistant concierges to the young men that sifted butts from the sand-filled ashtrays near the elevators. She suggested I go on vacation between December 15 and January 15. The first year anyway, I simply tipped everyone I knew. The following years, I took what I called the Hanff Hoofer and beat it out of town, much to the dismay of my friends and business partners. But I figured that I saved about $1500 each Christmas and used the time to make new contacts in the entertainment industry of which I was so much a part.

By 1993, I was actively interviewing Helene two times a week, but for periods no longer than two hours each. It was exhausting for her and I was getting more second hand smoke in the year that followed than all the rest of my life combined. I would bring lunch up with me. Her favorite was smoked turkey with Russian dressing and coleslaw on a crusty role with a new dill pickle all washed down with a bottle of Dr. Brown's Cel-Ray tonic, a drink which had been touted for decades about its healthy content of celery juice. The USDA forced the company to call it Cel-Ray (it used to be "Celery Tonic") when it was discovered that virtually no celery juice ever saw the interior of Dr. Brown's bottling plant. Admittedly, it was an acquired taste (like Helene's martinis) that offset the strong flavors of the kosher deli sandwiches I fastidiously delivered to her apartment. But it was a labor of love and I recorded over 150 hours of interviews along with nine spiral notebooks of notes about everything from her literary interests to her friends, her paramours and her family. It soon became obvious that the Helene Hanff of *84 Charing Cross Road* was indeed a creature of fiction touched only here and there by fact but that in essence there was not too much difference between the two if they were compared in a sober state. Invariably, by the time I had arrived at her apartment, half a pint of Beefeater gin had disappeared from a bottle she kept near her typewriter right next to a large boomeranged shaped blue plastic ashtray heaped with butts and ashes. Often there were two cigarettes lit at a time. One she had left by the kitchen sink while brewing a cup of Sanka (a decaffeinated instant concoction that resembles true coffee only in its color and the shape of the cup it is served in) and one in the ashtray by the typewriter.

As I got to meet the neighbors and the occasional relatives who dropped in over the course of time I was visiting; it was inevitable that I would by mere chance collide with them just by the sheer amount of time I spent with Helene. A third Helene emerged from talk with neighbors and a fourth evolved from interviews with relatives. I don't suppose any of this is uncommon, but I will say that the Helene portrayed so beautifully in the film by Anne Bancroft resembled none of the Helene's I came to know, but was an amalgam of all of them had I known each only fifteen minutes. Because of inconsistencies, some more important and obvious than others, I relate in this book both versions of stories or periods of time that were told to me. Biography is one of those art forms that require a very limited amount of creativity and a great deal of factual information. But because facts about people's relationships don't always mean absolute truth, I found it better to give multiple versions of the same story. I could have taken the position of judge and jury and simply made a ruling about who was telling the truth and who not. But I feel strongly that biography should be designed to elucidate and enlighten and be as objective as possible given those ideals. I'm reminded of a biography of Thomas Hardy by a friend of mine, Michael Millgate. His book relates only facts that he can provably demonstrate to be true either by reference to letters or other material evidence. Nothing is left for the creative side of writing. Another biographer, Seymour Smith, who deals in a huge volume with Hardy's life, takes a different approach. There is dialogue no one could have heard, facial expressions and physical gestures no one could have seen and intimate details no one could have or would have spoken of. His is the more interesting biography by far, but Millgate's clearly the more accurate. They both had the advantage of having a dead man as their subject matter; Hardy died in 1928, years before these two biographers even drew breath. Hardy himself wrote an autobiography in two volumes and made his second wife the author with instructions not to publish it until after his death. This she did, but not before editing out all the bits about his first wife where Hardy depicted her in a favorable light. Hardy thought by publishing his own story, he would preclude others from attempting it. He even asked that they not. So much for dying wishes. I have little doubt that Helene's many autobiographical books acted as a pre-emptive strike against people wanting to know more and I will say here and now that if you want the Helene Hanff of *84 Charing Cross Road*, read no further. Her books all carefully cultivate that tough-as-nails, warm-hearted individual persona with no personal life whatsoever. The truth is far different.

At the outset, Helene spoke to me like she did all of her fans, in a sort of "I know you think I'm terrific, warm, earnest and in every way just one of you; that my sentimentality is refreshing in a world gone amok. What's your name? I'll gladly sign the book." No one of her "fans," and she had lots of them, ever made it past the lobby of her building. Typically, she would meet them in the lobby and sit and chat and pose for a photo or two and then send them on their way, little red cartoon hearts popping out of their heads as they got out onto the streets of the Big Apple.

I soon learned that none of the letters that she sent to Marks and Co. existed anymore. She did not make copies and the recipients did not keep them or at least they were never discovered when the booksellers were shut down and evacuated their shop. The fact became clear that she had to re-write or more accurately, "re-create" her letters many years after they were written. More interestingly and quite apparent when they are read within the covers of the book, Helene does not evolve or mature over the course of the twenty years she was writing. Of course had they been the original letters, such would have been the case. But it took her a mere three months to reconstruct the letters by having their "shadows" interpreted by her use of the letters from Marks & Co, most, but not all of which, she had retained There are discrepancies throughout that prove this and some anachronistic details that a detailed reading would reveal. But I advise against it. Suffice to say that the book which so endears Helene Hanff to you should be read as a novel or one of those new-fangled ficto-biographies that seem so popular today, and not a mere collation of actual letters.

Helene was very careful to maintain a façade throughout the book that represented her as she wanted people to see her. It was never meant to be autobiographical and it was only my monthly payments to her—a topic I will discuss later—that produced the truth, if truth be the word—of the woman behind the typewriter. And certainly the Anne Bancroft of the film is as good a representation of Helene's façade as any that she herself could have manufactured although she balked at what she called the "cheesy poem by Yeats that some starry-eyed producer threw in" or the baleful expressions of Anthony Hopkins who "looked and acted as much like Frank Doel as J. Fred Muggs would have." (For the uninitiated, J. Fred Muggs was a 1950s TV celebrity that was a derby-wearing chimpanzee.)

Little fabrications, like receiving a "first edition" of Newman's *Idea of a University* never occurred. And had it occurred, the book would have been cloth bound not leather bound as she seems to swoon over in one of the letters. She did receive a cloth-bound later edition which she signed and gave to me. She loaned or misplaced the "little book" of Elizabethan love poetry that the employees sent her as a present; the letter that references it has the wrong title (her books were no more than five feet away from her typewriter.) Most interesting, despite her entreaties to the contrary, she was a huge fan of fiction and poetry and had all the great writers on her wood and cinder block shelves. (After the film royalties arrived, she replaced these with real mahogany bookcases.) I know; I inventoried them for her over a long weekend, hearing a story about each. Jane Austen, Charles Dickens, Burns, Browning, Matthew Arnold, Lewis Carroll, Edith Wharton, Virginia Woolf, Sue Grafton. They were all there; the great and the considerably less than great. It is true that when Helene drank she longed for the old days of the British Empire. She could recite Donne's sermons and Bacon's, whole sections of Hazlitt's essays. She loved historical truths told by people who were there. But she loved Jane Austen and a good mystery novel and even had a few copies of *Mad Magazine* lying about. Trollope and Shaw and Shakespeare could fill an afternoon. I remember one rainy November, at about 2 in the afternoon and only about ten minutes after the gin bottle had been emptied that she came out of the bathroom in a terry cloth bathrobe and did the death scene from *Antony and Cleopatra*—both roles. Her gravelly voice was perfect for Antony, but Cleopatra looked and sounded like a seventy year old drag queen. But I loved her for it and she was there, really there, in that tomb with Octavian's armies charging down a path to her pyramid. It was as if all the lost years of her life were beating down the door to her apartment and she was going to deprive them of their victory. She was, for a few minutes, the besieged Queen of the Nile and it was at that very moment that I truly understood Helene for the complex person she really was; not the wise-cracking American taking verbal jabs at a stodgy Brit 4000 miles away. She was defending her life and knew that this book would be a testament to the person she always wanted to be; except perhaps for the missing husband who was indeed an opera singer at the Brooklyn Academy of Music. It was a brief one-sided affair that was planted, took root, blossomed and died in a long autumn back in 1945. He was neither well-known nor particularly talented but he too loved the past. A whole fall season, she never missed a performance nor a rehearsal and it was only a dismal Thanksgiving in 1946 when she hoped he'd surprise her for dinner at her place that she discovered he was married. The betrayal threw her into a tailspin of self-denial, guilt and the sense that human beings were inherently wicked. It was John Donne that brought her from there out into the open. But her nerves were battered and her heart too broken to venture another relationship. This, I think, was unique to Helene—that she should pre-maturely abandon the hope of a meaningful relationship because of a heartbreaking jilting. But it is easy for the observer to preach. Each of us must mourn in our own way.

I've appended a list of books to the end of this biography, a list I had published earlier of books that make their appearance in *84 Charing Cross Road*. Along with every surface in her apartment—the walls, ceiling, furniture, pictures—her books were covered with a film of yellowish nicotine, tobacco residue. Every time I left her apartment, I had to disrobe the minute I got to my own apartment and put the clothes I wore in a plastic garbage bag—two actually—one for the dry cleaner and one for the washing machine. Anyone who has lived with a chain-smoker knows that the acrid smell of tobacco leeches into everything even remotely porous including skin and most particularly hair. Stripped and showered, I was ready to review my notes, transcribe important anecdotes and quotations, and organize a fairly ordinary life into some semblance of an explanation that squared with her books. It was more than interesting; it was a challenge I had encountered twice before: once for my bibliography of Sinclair Lewis and once for a bibliography of Theodore Dreiser. Both of these major writers were dead many decades and so much had been written about them that assembling relevant facts was simply that: an assemblage. But Helene Hanff was very much alive and her stories shifted like sands in the desert. At times she would go on and on about her opera singer; at other times, she denied even knowing an opera singer, saying instead that he was "a spear-holding extra." Sometimes, she was from a close family; other times, she was baffled by their indifference and hostility, often chalking up their disinterest in her to envy of her fame. The truth, as I hope to show, was a lot of both. For this reason, in most cases, I have changed the names, not to protect the innocent, but to ensure their privacy. No one of Helene's relatives at any time ever wanted to be named as a source. Now that many of them are dead, I am still duty bound to protect their privacy.

Helene had no photographs of friends or family anywhere in her apartment and it took me nearly a year to get up the courage to ask her to see any photo albums she might have had. "Photo albums?" she responded. "My photos are all up here" she added, pointing to her head. "And they change as the mood suits me. Isn't that the best kind of family?" I suppose this correlates with her denial in her books that she did not like fiction. In fact, she read every Jane Austen novel, most of Dickens and other Victorian novelists. I think this "factual" approach to presenting herself as someone grounded in historical reality takes her out of the realm of the creative and sentimental. How ironic is it that Jane Austen who writes exclusively about a woman finding the right man to marry, was Helene's favorite novelist? Helene never mentions a word in any of her books about any men in her life, let alone the "right" man. The unfortunate byproduct of her failure to speak about her love life has many people guessing that she was a lesbian. I suppose it is a product of our age that if you don't talk about one sex, you must be interested in the other. At no time did any evidence, material or hearsay, surface that indicates she was a homosexual.

Helene rarely wrote about her taste in music but it was amazingly conservative. She loved anything conducted by Leopold Stokowski and had written a short piece on his death entitled "Heartbreak Thursday" about showing up for a concert and it being canceled because of his unexpected demise. She loved Handel and Mozart and most chamber music but she despised jazz as "noisy and unstructured." It was around this time in the early 1990s that they had started digitally re-mastering older recordings and putting them on CDs. Helene had an old record player, an RCA one piece unit that played 33 1/3s, 45s and 78s. Most of her records were scratched and pretty well worn but she adored the tone of a needle on vinyl. When I brought up a CD player one afternoon and had her listen to a re-mastered Stokowski recording of *Night on Bald Mountain*, she listened attentively with a wry look in her eye. After it was over she said, "*Night on Bald Mountain?* It sounds like it was recorded on his bald head. Get that thing out of here." I did and, usually at some holiday, I visited an old record store downtown called Vinyl-Mania and bought her slightly used recordings of her favorites. I turned her on to my favorite British composer, Ralph Vaughn-Williams which she often listened to late into the night as she once told me, imagining the English countryside as John Donne must have seen it. As for the 1960s British wave of rock that crashed on American shores, in particular the Beatles, she quipped, "They're cute but that music! My God, it's so cute it could give you diabetes. I like the hair. It reminds me of a picture of my father's sister only hers was shorter. Don't they have barbers in London or Liverpool or wherever these lads are from?" Eventually she embraced the Beatles, the Rolling Stones and a group called the Zombies. But I never believed for a minute that it was anything but Helene's way of appearing liberal and "progressive" and that she was a closet classics lover who could tolerate little else. But she did listen continuously, mainly late at night, and when her turntable finally gave out, it took a week and $160.00 to get it repaired. I stocked up on "cartridges" for her—the little part at the end of the tone arm that holds the needle. Except for nightclub usage, no one was manufacturing turntables anymore, let alone parts. Only recently has vinyl made a feeble comeback. Her records ended up in the garbage chute at her building as her relatives discarded everything they thought had no value. Maybe they were right, but I wish I had gotten a few of them. It would be great to kick back and listen to Stokowski conduct the Messiah and sip a martini and smoke a Marlboro—not inhaling of course.

Helene always led a paycheck-to-paycheck existence and managed to eek out a living writing an occasional junior high school text book or a column for a small left-leaning newspaper or *The Readers Digest*. Her job as novel reader provided almost no income but she made light talk of it in one of her autobiographies. These books, *The Duchess of Bloomsbury Street, Letters from New York, Apple of My Eye* and *Q's Legacy* are so filled with fictional material that they can be said to be more like novels than factual accounts of her life. The manuscript for her first volume, *Underfoot in Show Business,* was originally only about twenty pages in typed length. A ghost writer was retained to flesh out Helene's meager experiences on Broadway, most of which she did not want to discuss. But rather than have someone else do it, she revised and enlarged the volume herself. It may be surprising that someone who wrote so much about her life revealed so little. And it was not a matter of keeping her admiring public wanting more; she was an intensely private person who sought out writing as a way to pay her bills and if the public wanted to hear stories about her life, they'd have to settle for the highly abridged and mostly fabricated versions which appeared in print. The anecdotes are all told as if they involved someone else. Her objectivity and self-deprecating sense of humor is endearing but it also functions to hide anything negative that happened to her or anything too personal. The wry, comedic tone of the books squares with the persona portrayed in *84 Charing Cross Road.* All of them are devoid of emotion. The film of *84* ends not with a tearful "Hello" to the ghosts of the empty bookshop but the quip, "Well, Frankie, I finally made it." Admittedly, this is much closer to how she really felt than most of her readers would like to think. In her post-84 book, *The Duchess of Bloomsbury Street,* she apologizes in the first chapter for being able to visit only after Frank Doel died. It was his death that gave her the idea to publish the letters, originally as a magazine article, and then as a novel at the insistence of Grossman Publishing in New York.

She did not, unfortunately, believe in lawyers and when her various publishers sent over their form agreement, a lopsided and grotesquely unfair contract for her to sign, she simply signed. Perhaps they were expecting a lawyer to represent her and offered less with the expectation of him negotiating for more. This never happened. She made an offhand comment in one of her books how people sent her copies of her books to sign without enclosing return postage and that in mailing them back, she was losing money on the deal. Both Grossman and later Moyer Bell, paid her so little on the continuous sale of her books that had she sold ten times the number of copies, she would still have been dependent on social security and the kindness of strangers. Even the movie rights to *84* were so paltry that all she could wring out of it was a trip to London with meals and lodging, some of which were paid for by a "mysterious" friend whose name never materialized, and some new furniture. When I spoke to Moyer Bell Publishing in 1999, they were so secretive about Helene that it aroused more suspicions than it resolved. Her publishers uniformly took the public position that they were being protective of their helpless, non-business-oriented author. "Like most authors," they said, "Helene just could not handle money matters." They watched over her like the proverbial fox watching over the hen house. According to her, while Helene's book sales continued over decades, the royalties stayed the same, an unusual agreement if there ever was one; no factoring in of inflation or increased popularity with decreased costs. I would estimate that Helene had about six different outfits to wear, two pairs of shoes, a pair of slippers, a robe, and an overcoat that the moths enjoyed as much as she enjoyed her smokes. And yes, a black/brown cashmere sweater that would have been discarded had it been in a thrift shop. At some point, though, she managed to refurnish her apartment.

We generally consider Helene Hanff to have been a political liberal and it is true that she always voted Democrat. But in those days, the 1930s to the 1980s, liberalism was much more conservative than it has been painted today. Nonetheless, she was always a dyed-in-the-wool Democrat who even voted for Hubert Humphrey despite the fact that when she was arrested for the Columbia University sit-in protesting the Vietnam War. It was a war started and enlarged by Kennedy and Johnson and there was no doubt in anyone's mind that Johnson's Vice President, Hubert H. Humphrey would keep us mired in the jungles for as long as it took to win what was an unwinable war, very much like the current wars in Iraq and Afghanistan. The student riots of the late 1960s were directed against the Democrat establishment, something Helene avoided talking about even in *The Movers and Shakers*, her only foray into political writing. The moving and shaking she referred to was the far left movements of civil rights and isolationist foreign policy reflected in a stop-the-war policy. I know.

I was there and would have voted for Genghis Khan if he promised to save my butt by not drafting me to be cannon-fodder in a jungle I knew nothing about and cared even less for. All that "moving and shaking" gave the United States Richard Nixon as president. The rest is history.

As a general rule, I let her autobiographical books speak for themselves; I do not wish to re-hash material she covered so well and there is nothing within those books that reveals anything she was not more than happy to reveal. I avoid contradicting them unless the evidence is overwhelming. This was, fortunately, rarely the case and so I have not duplicated anecdotes that she relates so enthusiastically. She, too, altered names to protect people's privacy and it came as quite a surprise when she told me the real names of the staff at Marks & Co. Those people she could reach before publication, she asked permission for the use of their real names. Those she could not, she fabricated names for. Of course, she had to seek permission to publish Frank Doel's letters to her. Copyright law dictates that while the recipient of a letter owns the letter, the writer retains the copyright. As Doel was deceased when Helene wrote *84*, the copyright passed to his estate, in this case to his wife. Between January of 1969 when she was informed of Frank Doel's death and October, 1969, she wrote at least two letters to Sheila Doel seeking permission to use the letters in her book. Oddly, while she included her letter to Sheila expressing her regrets at Frank's death, she did not include the letters asking permission to print his letters which Nora graciously granted. It is a tradition in British literature to include the letter from the copyright owner granting permission as a "stamp of approval" to reprint a writing; this is very common where non-English books are translated and published. Sheila gladly gave permission for Helene to publish them, probably and understandably not foreseeing the value that copyright held; Nora Doel received nothing, even surrendering inadvertently the movie rights (along with the Broadway and London stage rights.) Since its first appearance in 1970, on both sides of the Atlantic and in many other languages, *84 Charing Cross Road* has never been out of print and numerous community theater groups put on the play many times in the course of a year. Brian Bainbridge, a close friend of the Doels, received a note from Sheila concerning Helene's request:

"Sheila was in the midst of tidying up Frank's estate which was by no means an easy task. There were many letters of condolence that needed answering and gifts of flowers, etc. Because of Frank's intimate relationship with Marks & Co., and the death of Mr. Marks so close in time to his own, there were several questions raised by solicitors as to who owned what books; Frank was known to collect books himself and some unfortunately were left in the shop. There was also the matter of a possible malpractice action against his physicians, it being uncommon to die from appendicitis. Amidst all this, Miss Hanff was pleading her case for the publication of Frank's letters. It was unseemly, in my opinion, in view of what the Doels were going through. But Sheila and Nora more by way of getting rid of the problem than resolving it sensibly, yielded to her requests. I personally think it was a mistake. And I so informed Sheila and Nora, but neither would have any of it and that was that."

By the terms of Helene's will, Arlene Wolff (and her estate) receives the royalty payments. Because I was unaware of this arrangement at the time of my interviews, I never had the opportunity to enquire of Helene the motive for this bequest. It seems to me that the Doels should have received half, if not all of the royalties upon Helene's death. After all, Frank Doel wrote half the book that made Helene Hanff the famous author she became.

When I spoke at a Popular Culture Conference on Helene Hanff, I told everyone that the one thing that Helene did was to encourage reading of all kinds. I think most of her fans identify with this idea. Every Hanff fan I've ever met or e-mailed or talked to on the phone is an avid reader and what I found was that most of these fans liked Helene because she was a book reader first and a book collector second. There is a common and accurate perception that most book collectors do not read the books they collect, which is usually true. That is not to say that they haven't read a paperback copy of, for example, *The Great Gatsby*. They might collect a first edition of *Gatsby* but they would not read it because it costs somewhere between fifty and a hundred thousand dollars in its original dustwrapper. If you want to read the Bible, you don't read the Dead Sea Scrolls and leave them on your nightstand. Most collectors are very familiar with the text of the books they collect.

Helene revealed a more interesting side to her notion of reading in *Underfoot in Show Business* which was published before *84 Charing Cross Road* and therefore, before she was established as the patron saint of the reading common man (as one of her UK admirers put on her website.)

"I got so I could read a long novel in an evening and write the summary in half an hour before breakfast. I keep hearing about these college courses that will teach you how to read faster; don't take them. I'll give you the whole course right here for free. Here's how to read *War and Peace* in three hours: Run your eyes down the left hand side of the page, stopping at the first line of each paragraph . . . .Just keep running your eye down until you come to a paragraph where something *happens*. In the average novel, such a paragraph will turn up on one page in every twenty-five at most."

Helene's advice: skim. In this regard, the details of her life are a skim. I have pieced together all that I could. This book is episodic and anecdotal and almost all of it is from Helene herself as few others were willing or able to speak about her. Sometimes, her recollections seem more creative than realistic but she was most definitely a truthful and direct person. Anything she did not want people to know about, she remained silent on. If there are fabrications, I could not evaluate them and third party sources, as I have said, were non-existent.

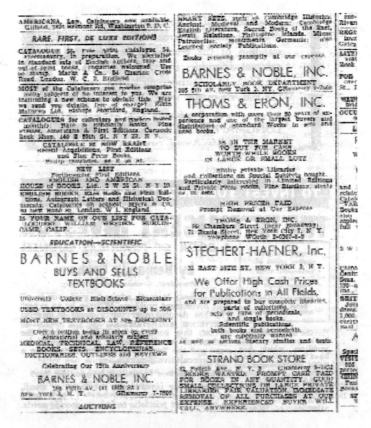

New York Times Book Review, Oct 2, 1949

IT BEGINS

She had been up until 2:30 in the morning. Something inside her said to gather together all the letters she had received and diligently saved since the winter of 1949. Most of them she had squirreled away in a dusty blue cardboard accordion folder with a frayed string tie that didn't quite make it all around. There were about fifty letters in the folder, mostly out of chronological order, some with their envelopes with the oddly pretty British stamps, all with Queen Elizabeth's portrait, but some, the early ones, with George the VI, in dapper and handsome profile. Unfortunately, there were some missing and she looked everywhere, even in the flattened cartons she kept under her bed filled with clothes that were out of season. Two letters were in a wool sack purse. That was good. She found two more on the shelf in the only closet under a hatbox that held her one good hat: a wide-brimmed felt number her friend Maxine had given her just after the war. Three more were in a box marked "stationery" and another one was crumpled up in a pile of old, but thankfully paid Con Edison electric bills.

Helene methodically put all the letters in thin but very neat piles, year by year, starting in 1949 and ending in 1970. She then made one pile of them, placed them on her desk, finished the watered down gin she had started at 11:00 and went to sleep.

The next morning, the third cup of coffee went down quickly. Helene gulped a bit as the java without sugar or cream was a little hotter than she expected. It was a fitting partner to her fourth cigarette hanging unlit from her lips.

The February sun was thin and wan; it angled through the window and barely lit up the corner of Helene Hanff's studio apartment. For an hour or so, it meandered across the floor, highlighting the nap of the worn olive-green rug. It crept up the cement block and red mahogany bookshelves that lined one wall where neat rows of shabby books stood silently. The Sunday *New York Times* was in a corner by the door, thoroughly read, most of it.

She lit the cigarette and looked out the window scanning the bright morning sky indifferently lighting the rooftops and water storage towers of her East 72d Street neighborhood. Bus brakes squealed and the muted horns of taxicabs beeped subtle tunes at every corner and crosswalk in the neighborhood. It wasn't blue jays and robins, but it was what she wanted and loved. Helene was a city girl—well perhaps not a girl anymore at age 55—but she was a city girl, a New York City girl through and through. The bucolic joys of lawns, trees, foraging deer and the early morning sounds of school buses held no allure to her. She was in love with New York and, sitting in her slip at 10:45 AM that morning, she was still under the spell of the Big Apple.

She sat in front of her 25 year old typewriter and began pecking away at the keys in her usual frenetic fashion. Her coffee cup blotted out another rejection slip she had received a few weeks earlier; near it was a letter from one of the Marks & Co., Booksellers, London, employees informing her of the death of her longtime "pen pal" Frank Doel, the store's manager.

"Dear Daphne," she wrote to Daphne Carr of Marks & Co., London. "I do hope dear Frank's funeral went without a hitch and that he is lying in peace. I'm so terribly sorry I missed his final farewell, but we were never ones to make too much of a sad ending anyway. Might I ask you a favor?" she continued, "please look in the files if you get a moment and see if the letters I've written him are anywhere to be found. I'm certain he's kept them somewhere—perhaps with the receipts of my purchases. Let me know what you've found, even if it's nothing at all. I'm missing him and would love to reminisce. With all my love to everyone there, Helene."

She pulled the missive out of the typewriter, hand signed her own name over the typed one and admired again her tasteful blue-bordered stationery and the sedate typeface of her name and address engraved at the top.

"This could be the start of something," she said to herself. She slipped on a chenille bathrobe, walked to the door of her flat, adjusted the lock so she wouldn't need the key and made her way down the dimly lit hallway to the elevator.

"Good morning, Helene," startled her from her reverie.

"Good morning, Harriet . . . Geez, you made me jump. I'm still half asleep"

"If you're going down to get the mail, you're way too early," Harriet replied from her half open doorway. Helene could smell the greasy smoke of burnt fried eggs coming from Harriet Moulton's apartment.

"Nope. I'm posting a letter myself. Thanks for the warning."

"Think nothing of it," Harriet replied.

The elevator door opened and all the way down to the lobby, she mused about the letters she had written to Marks & Co. She reached the main floor where the long row of tarnished mailboxes occupied one full wall. She was suddenly flooded with memories of the letters and parcels she had received there over the past two decades, each one a joyous interlude in a hand-to-mouth life. She placed the letter in the "Out Box."

"With any luck," she said out loud. "Dear old FPD held on to them. If he didn't, that's okay, too."

Helene's Typewriter with Marks & Co. Receipt

CHAPTER 1

SP: I'd like to start by asking how much you remember about your visit to the former bookshop space at 84 Charing Cross Road.

HH: Like it was yesterday. Which to my mind it was [laughing].

SP: How so?

HH: Well you know it was in terrible shape. Not like in the film at all. There was rubble all over the place and it wasn't helped by promotional people and photographers. I got snapped too many times for comfort.

SP: Did you sense the presence of the staff at least?

HH: Not at all. It was an old store that was being gutted to make way for I think a burger joint. The shelves were in a heap. At least I think they were shelves. They might have been bits of paneling. The partitions were gone. It was a mess, plain and simple. Even the windows were covered with brown paper. There was no sense whatsoever that it had been a book store. Hardly a dramatic reunion.

SP: So it was dramatized for the film then?

HH: Dramatized? It was completely fictionalized. But you know that's OK. Things change. Buildings get torn down and rebuilt. Where we're sitting right now there was probably a beautiful row of brownstones with flower boxes and wrought-iron rails out front. Every neighborhood changes over time. Time stands still for no one, you know. And it shouldn't. Nostalgia is what sells because it makes people think you can go home again. It was Thomas Wolff said that, wasn't it?

SP: It was.

HH: You can't go home again. I think what touched people about *84* was the idea that you could, that there was a kinder, gentler time. Well, there wasn't because every time was what it was and the people that lived then thought it was better before they were there. I read a book once that Arlene gave me. It was called—and don't hold me to it—*The Good Old Days; They Were Terrible*. I don't think that's true but would I want to live in John Donne's England? Maybe for a day or two. Disease, crime, political intrigue, people disappearing in the middle of the night because they said something wrong at dinner. No thanks. And besides, I'm a Jew. Can you imagine a nice Jewish girl trying to hoof it in merry old England? Remember Rebecca in *The Master of Ballantrae?*

SP: I think it was *Ivanhoe,* but I do remember.

HH: She was beautiful—played by Liz Taylor in the movie—even she would've been burned at the stake. Look, honey, we can all dream a bit. It's good for the soul. Some pick the future, some pick the past. I love history; always did. But it's not real. Not like we want to think. We project our own priorities, our own likes and dislikes into it. Nothing is real unless you live it. Anything else is fiction, pure and simple.

SP: So would you say your book *84 Charing Cross Road* is fiction?

HH: I knew that was coming. [Takes a sip of gin]. Of course it is. I mean the letters you and I both know were mostly fictionalized for obvious reasons. But those years were not good ones. I didn't know where my next meal was coming from sometimes. And I must tell you, it was lonely. That's something people don't realize. I made the best of it. But it was lonely. Sure, there were good times occasionally but if you read my books carefully, years had gone by between some of those letters. Well, not always years, but months definitely. A lot of months. Most of it is a long blur. Someone talked about people leading lives of quiet desperation. That sums it up. People like to think that Doel and I were sitting by the mailbox waiting for each other's letters. It wasn't like that at all. I didn't think about Marks & Co. for long stretches. And if he thought about me . . . well, he would have been wasting his time. I guess book people have a lot of time to waste, though.

SP: I think you're right. If you consider reading a waste of time.

HH: Ha! That's a laugh. No, I won't say that but show me a guy making a million bucks a year and if he has time to read the TV Guide, I'd be surprised.

SP: I think you're right.

HH: Of course you do. You make a good living—actually a very good living—how many books do you read, not counting taking one into the bathroom with you?

SP: Actually, without the toilet, I don't think I'd finish a book in a year.

HH: Case closed. Who's next on the docket?

Helene Hanff was a sixth generation American with ancestors that arrived from Great Britain shortly after the Revolutionary War. Her great-great-grandmother, Mary Bailey, was born of English Quaker parents in Philadelphia in 1807. Sometime between 1821 and 1824, she married a Portuguese seaman, Emmanuel Semon, who had made his way to the "New World" by working as a ship's cook from Portugal to Holland and then finally to the United States. The Semons settled in Richmond, Virginia and raised seventeen children—all of whom lived to adulthood.

In 1848, one of their daughters, Tabitha, married a Bavarian Jew, Jacob Bacharach, who had emigrated to America with his parents only a few years earlier. His heavy Yiddish-German accent amused Tabitha, but her father made Jacob promise that he would learn English fluently, drop his old world ways and raise the children as good, Southern Americans.

When the War Between the States broke out in 1861, the Bacharachs were staunch Confederate supporters. Jacob worked at one of the few munitions factories in the South and was trusted with packing and shipping arms to General Lee's army. As the war progressed, it became apparent that the North would likely prevail and Jacob asked his employers to be paid in bullion as he felt the paper money of the Confederacy would be worth less after the war than it seemed to be in 1864. He was refused and he decided that despite his fierce support of the cause, he would make his way elsewhere. He purchased a small farm near Charlottesville, Virginia in 1865, just in time to see the war's end. A few lean years later, the birth of his first daughter, Caroline, in 1872 brought him the first rays of hope and he died a fairly wealthy landowner in 1887, survived by three children.

Caroline married into her Jewish faith in 1890. A handsome and conservative Philadelphian named Elias Hanff proposed to her within weeks of their meeting at synagogue. Within four years, they had two children, a son, Arthur (born 1892) and a daughter, Cecile (born 1894). Elias worked the family cotton business with Caroline's brothers, Bernard and David.

Just after the turn of the twentieth century, when Arthur and Cecile were teenagers, the family for unknown reasons moved to Philadelphia; family stories held that the rise of the Ku Klux Klan had singled them out as Jews and Elias was not going to take any chances. In the early months of January, 1901 they made their way to a house Jacob had purchased with proceeds he received for his share of the business a few months earlier. Without knowing it, the neat brick house was located only three doors down from where Mary Bailey had lived a century earlier.

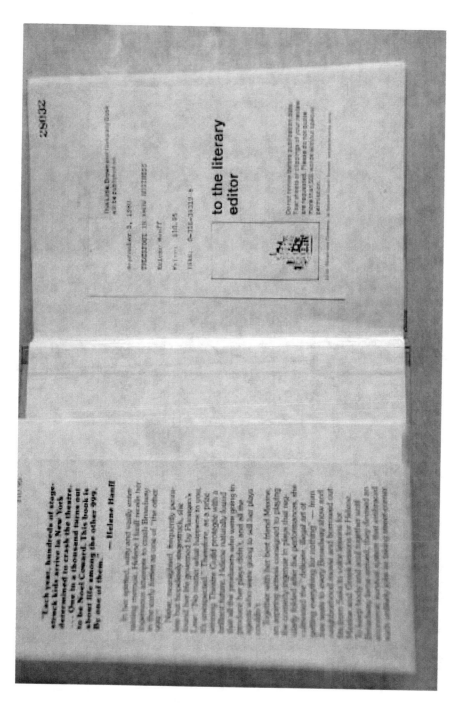

Review Copy in Helene's Library

Arthur Hanff

CHAPTER 2

SP: What was the high point of your life?

HH: That's a dumb question.

SP: Thanks.

HH: You're welcome. But seriously, who can say? It depends.

SP: On what?

HH: On a lot of things. But off the top of my head, I'd say meeting Anne Bancroft. What a delightful person. Down to earth, intelligent, sensitive, sweet.

SP: That's what a good many people say about you.

HH: Well they're right. [Laughing] Mostly anyway. No, I can safely say that Anne was a wonder. I could tell she was genuine the minute I met her. The real deal. Not a Hollywood bone in her body. Look, she's married to Mel Brooks. How much does that tell you? A nicer couple you couldn't imagine.

SP: Were you flattered by her playing you?

HH: No, it should have been Whoopi Goldberg. Of course, I was flattered. It only took them four hours a day to make her look ugly.

SP: [laughing] I heard it was six hours.

HH: So now you're a comedian?

Elias Hanff's son, Arthur, did not have the same conservative political or religious bent as his father. While Elias had hopes of Arthur going into the burgeoning field of commodities trading, Arthur was hell-bent on a career on the stage. Arthur Hanff spent every spare penny on tickets to the Vaudeville. It was the golden age of this Broadway pre-cursor and the bright lights, slapstick buffoons, happy throngs and beautiful dancing girls held him in their sway. By the time he was seventeen, Arthur Hanff wanted a career in show business. He would do just about anything to get a break.

His first job was at a small theatre on Chestnut Street, the Orpheum, where he swept floors, cleaned dressing rooms and erased the big star names on the chalkboard schedule every vaudeville theatre had, listing the order of the acts for all employees to see. He wanted his name there (he occasionally put "Artie Hanff" as the "lead act" just to see how it looked) and any free time he had was spent tap dancing and singing on an empty poorly lit stage to a dark theatre. Ivan Jensen, a recent Norwegian émigré, became his best friend and provided a single pair of hands to applaud Arthur's dancing and his garbled version of Abbie's Irish Rose.

One evening, just before Christmas of 1908, Arthur was cleaning up as usual, pushing a large dust mop around the well-worn boards of the stage. Johnston Smith, the Orpheum's booking agent came in to the theatre and, lighting a cigarette, stood in the wings and watched Arthur. Arthur made small talk about the acts that were on stage that night and Smith listened, adding his own comments here and there as to who he thought would go on to bigger and better things and who wouldn't. He asked Arthur what a good-looking lad like him was doing pushing a broom. Arthur replied that this was his way of breaking in to show business—after all, he didn't know anyone. Smith said that he did now. Arthur auditioned right there and then at Smith's request, singing and dancing to the band that only Arthur could hear in his head.

Smith politely told him that his act, such as it was, needed "polishing" and that the way to do it was not to be cleaning washrooms, but to be performing in venues out West. Almost every big star had started in some one-horse town west of the Mississippi early on and he could see no reason for Arthur to do any differently.

The next day, Arthur got a note of introduction and a five dollar bill for train fare out to the Wyatt Downs Dance Hall in Redding, Montana, population 2,127, a stone's throw from Helena, which Arthur later told Helene, was the source of her name, but that the nurse at Union Hospital (where Helene was born six years later) had spelled it incorrectly. The note from Smith also said that if Arthur made it to the East Coast stage, he expected his usual fifteen percent.

"Papa" Hanff made the traditional and expected objections but he knew that his son had to follow "his star." Privately he confided in Arthur's mother (with his resonant trilled Rs) that Arthur would be back in Philadelphia in "trrree weeks, maybe less, if the trrrain is rrrunning." So, with his parents' apparent blessings, Arthur packed a valise, kissed his sister Cecile goodbye and headed for the train station. He arrived in Redding seven days later with his suit rumpled and stained, but his spirits soaring.

His first "gig" was as a back-up singer to a minstrel act in black face. Arthur had to learn a few tunes on a beat up banjo and learned to "mug." It was six months later that the lead in his act failed to show for curtain call and Arthur had his big break. He became the lead and a 14 year old stage hand with the unlikely name of Sebastian Sebastian became his back-up. This was not what Arthur had in mind for a career, but he kept at it hoping that better things were ahead. At least, he thought, he was on the stage and not just cleaning it.

Arthur Hanff's stint in Montana came to an abrupt end when the hall's owner was shot and killed during a poker game. He wasn't playing poker and wasn't even at the table, but a stray shot from an upraised gun held by a drunk who was playing poker killed Arthur's meal ticket. The next day, Arthur packed his bag and, with Sebastian Sebastian in tow, headed to Jackson Hole, Wyoming.

New Year's day, 1910 passed without notice as Arthur and his friend slept in their twenty five cent seats in the train on the way to a town with an apt name; Jackson Hole had a huge hole, a silver mine with miners who filled the local theatre seven days a week, twice on Sunday. The aptly named Real Nugget Saloon would separate the real nuggets from the fool's gold.

Miriam Levy

CHAPTER 3

SP: I'm going to ask some personal questions. Feel free to be honest.

HH: Very funny. If it's honesty you want, try talking to the Dalai Lama.

SP: I tried. But I have a bad knee and climbing that mountain was more than I could handle.

HH: That's a good one. So what do you want to know?

SP: Why did you never marry?

HH: Is that a proposal?

SP: In another life maybe.

HH: I can wait.

SP: No, Helene, seriously, enquiring minds want to know.

HH: Enquiring minds need to ask more important questions.

SP: You have a good many fans out there. Most of them are women. And I guess it's only natural for them to wonder why an intelligent, accomplished, attractive woman like yourself never got hitched?

HH: I guess the right man never came along. I mean what can you expect me to say. There was love in my life. Deep, meaningful love. Even passion. But, you know, it's not easy to find the right person. Or to have him find you. In those days, women were not as forward as they are today. Maybe I looked too hard, thought too much. I saw too many bad marriages around me. And in those days you couldn't just dial 1-800-DIVORCE. It was a major commitment and, thinking back, which I do, maybe I took it all too seriously. I was never one for risk. You know I never learned to swim?

SP: Why not?

HH: My mother had a friend whose son drowned in a swimming hole. She figured that if I didn't know how to swim, I wouldn't go in the water and if I didn't go in the water, I wouldn't drown.

SP: Interesting.

HH: She was right. I never drowned.

It wasn't long before Sebastian found better work, more lucrative at any rate, in the silver mines. Arthur, however, was a man on a mission and money, or the lack thereof, was not going to derail his dream. It would take more than that.

Enter, Sandra Stemple. Sandra was an attractive red-haired, buxom chorus girl at the Real Nugget. She also had a daughter by the name of Margaret. The father was, purportedly, John "Woody" Woodruff, the owner of the Real Nugget Saloon. Within a few weeks, and noticing that Arthur had an eye for the 18 year old Sandra, Woody approached Arthur with a proposition: if Arthur married Sandra, he would receive fifty dollars (ten weeks salary). Of course, if Arthur accepted the offer, he would have to leave the employ of the Real Nugget. If he didn't accept, he'd be fired anyway. Thus in a corner, Arthur wisely accepted the fifty dollars, Margaret unwisely, perhaps, accepted Arthur's "proposal" and, on August 12, 1910, they were married in front of a Justice of the Peace.

Arthur, his bride and her daughter all quickly packed up and left town to work for Samuel Woodruff, Woody's older brother who owned the Nantucket Inn, a bar and brothel, in Jarred, Wyoming (population 700), about fifty miles south/southwest of Jackson Hole.

At the Nantucket Inn, Arthur played the honky-tonk piano and Sandra was a barmaid. Jarred bordered an Indian reservation and several members of the Nez Perce Indian tribe of the Wasatch Mountain range were regular customers of the Nantucket Inn. Between sets, Arthur would stand out front and watch the comings and goings of the raucous frontier town. It was on the front porch that he met the 16 year old daughter of one of the Nantucket Inn's Nez Perce customers. In a small town like Jared, word that Arthur had taken up with an Indian girl reached Sandra's ears and Arthur woke one night to find Sandra hovering over him with a knife to his throat. Right then and there, he vowed to give up the girl and get another job so that the couple could move out of the Inn into their own house, preferably in another town. Margaret, by this time was six years old and the time had come for the family to move to more respectable lodgings.

Clearly, it was evident to Arthur that show business, at least as it was then, did not have a place for him. Under the pretext of finding work and housing in Helena, Arthur boarded the train with satchel in hand and never looked back. What meager possessions and money the couple had accumulated, he left with Sandra and Margaret. Whatever guilt he may have felt for leaving them to fend for themselves, he never revealed to anyone. It wasn't until after his death that anyone discovered that he had been married in Wyoming, legally making him a bigamist when he married Helene's mother and that under the laws of every state at that time, any children of a subsequent marriage would be bastards.

The train, with Arthur on it, made its way across the bleak and snow-driven plains of the Midwest in December, 1911 toward Philadelphia. The United States was recovering from a deep recession, Europe was showing early signs of political upheaval in the Balkans, but Arthur Hanff, now 19 years old, had only the thought of being home for Hanukkah on his mind and wondering what lay ahead after that.

Helene Hanff, August 1916

CHAPTER 4

SP: It's nice to get an early start.

HH: For you, maybe. I'm not a morning person.

SP: I wanted to ask you about your fans. I remember your writing that people would send their books to you for a signature or an inscription and they wouldn't enclose return postage. And that you'd lose money on the book because the royalty was less than the postage.

HH: I'm afraid that's true. I trust people almost to a fault and it does usually work out for me but every now and then, it doesn't. I'd rather lead a life of trust and not think everyone is out to get me than to double think people. That would take most of the joy out of life.

SP: I agree. I'm trusting too and in my line of work, it rarely works out but I don't want to end up a paranoid. Are you intimating that your royalties were not what they should be?

HH: I don't think I want to go there. They are what they are and I'm grateful.

SP: Well, how about your fans?

HH: They're terrific. Sometimes they're a lifeline for me.

SP: What do you mean?

HH: I know there are people out there I can reach out to. They are like friends.

SP: They get to know you through your books?

HH: Of course.

SP: Isn't that a lot like your relationship with Frank Doel? Long distance.

HH: How so? Are you a shrink?

SP: No, most definitely not. I don't believe in therapists or psychiatrists.

HH: You should try it.

SP: Maybe it would help me to understand why people keep ducking questions.

HH: Touché.

SP: So you were talking about your fans.

HH: And I said they're great. Which they are.

SP: I know a few have come to visit.

HH: They have.

SP: For lunch? Dinner?

HH: I don't have them come up here.

SP: Why not?

HH: Because you never know. I'm a New Yorker. If I let everyone I meet into my apartment, God only knows what could happen. But actually, I want to be able to get up and leave. If I couldn't do that, I'd have to say, 'Would you mind leaving; I'm a bit tired.' I wouldn't want to do that. But some of these people who are quite wonderful would talk for days. So in the lobby, I can say, 'Gotta go. See ya.' And no one gets offended. So that's why the lobby is a perfect middle ground. Other times I talk on the phone with them. My number is listed. I've got a number of people who admire my work in the UK. The telephone is a great invention and I've never heard of anyone getting robbed over the phone.

SP: Isn't that a little contradictory with your statement about trusting everyone?

HH: I'm a writer. If I want to contradict myself, it's allowed.

Isaac and Ruth Levy had recently moved from Mott Street in New York City's Lower East Side to Philadelphia. They had two children, a son, Jacob (later called Albert) and a daughter, Miriam. (Helene, in a rare reference to her family roots always referred to the Levys as the "Biblical" side of the family. She once confided that there were times in her life when she firmly believed that the name "Job" would have been more appropriate for her than Helene.) Miriam was a clerk in a small bookshop in Philadelphia where she would soon meet Arthur.

Family anecdotes that originated with a brief line in *Q's Legacy*, have Arthur showing up in Philadelphia lice-ridden and impoverished, getting a hot bath from his mother and having his clothes burned. Helene had said she had heard this from her Aunt Cecile, but then revised the story to his simply returning home with a "hopeless feeling" about any possibilities of a career on the stage. At 19 years of age, it would have been most unusual and equally unnecessary for his mother to "bathe him." Nonetheless, as many of Helene's written "recollections," this seems to be a bit of a stretch with an added dash of poetic license.

Within weeks of returning home, Arthur obtained a position as a deliveryman for a courier firm. Taking a parcel to the Witherspoon & Sons, Booksellers, he met Miriam. Always with an eye for the ladies, her striking slim figure and long jet black hair done up in a fashionable "French twist," Miriam caught his rapt attention. Their courtship lasted a mere six months, moments by the standards of the day, and they were duly married in a Jewish ceremony on July 12, 1912.

Ten months later, May 17, 1913, Arthur J. Hanff, Jr. was born. Much consternation was aroused by the naming of Arthur, Jr. after his father. Jewish custom prohibits the naming of a child after a living forebear. Miriam and Arthur were adamant about the naming and the distancing of the Hanff family from its Jewish roots had begun.

A year to the day later, a second son, Edward was born, May 17, 1914. And on April 15, 1916, Helene Marjorie Hanff was born to the Arthur Hanffs of Philadelphia.

Helene was not known or remembered by her family as a remarkable child in any way. But she was lovingly cared for and she thrived in a household full of the attention that the youngest and only female child would naturally receive. While her parents indulged all three children with playthings, such as were available in those times, Helene was content as a small child of four or five years, to sit in the kitchen at her mother's feet and play with the pots and pans she could reach in the low cupboards and the potatoes that were stored under the sink. She would sit for hours putting potatoes in the pots and removing them again. It was also her habit to do this when visiting friends and relatives. On one occasion, when Arthur and his family visited his parents for Sunday dinner, Helene was sternly told by Miriam prior to the visit not to touch the pots and potatoes. When Grandmother Levy opened the door to the family, Helene stepped forward without saying hello and announced, "Don't worry, Grandmother, I won't play with your pots and potatoes . . . " Grandmother Hanff swept little Helene up into her arms, took her to the kitchen and pulled out every pot and potato she had and said, "Here they are my sweet child, my darling, play all you want!"

By the summer of 1925, Arthur, Sr. had been promoted to "Scheduling and Employment Manager" at the courier service, but his salary was still too meager to allow them to purchase a home of their own. Arthur approached his mother's brother, Uncle Albert (nee Jacob) for advice. Uncle Al, as he was called in later years, was a "rich uncle" who was a successful stock broker on the Philadelphia Stock Exchange. Uncle Al set up an interview with the Arrow Shirt Company and Arthur was immediately hired; his salary increased with room to rise in a large and fiscally solid company.

Arthur's territory for selling the fine shirts of the Arrow Shirt Company included southeastern Pennsylvania, northern New Jersey and New York City. He would be on his route for short stints of four or five days, but it didn't take long for rumors to circulate that Arthur had a "lady friend" in Manhattan and another in Hoboken, New Jersey.

Arthur's success as a salesman, likely based in large part on his abilities as a stage performer, earned him commissions substantial enough to allow the family to purchase a 3 storey walk-up row house in a middle-class neighborhood. Helene's memories of her parents' heated "discussions" about the other women in Arthur's life were sketchy and painful. She was just reaching adolescence with all the attendant stresses of that stage of life and she tried as best she could to blot out the stream of invective she would hear through her parents' bedroom door "coiling like a snake," as she put it later in life, down the central stairwell that joined all three floors of the family home. In an effort at escapism and, to some degree to please a favorite history teacher she had that year, one Mrs. Bailey, she lost herself in extensive readings of fifteenth and sixteenth century England and Colonial America. It was during this time that she developed her love of England and all things British.

On October 29, 1929 the bottom fell out of the economic universe. Worldwide financial markets collapsed and just about everyone the Hanffs knew were affected. Arthur's skill and success as a salesman insured his being kept on at the shirt company, but many of his colleagues lost their positions as markets dried up over the ensuing months. Rich Uncle Al, who was heavily margined in the market, lost everything. Arthur came to the rescue, not forgetting that it was Uncle Al who helped Arthur gain his place at Arrow. Albert Levy, still a bachelor, moved in to the spare bedroom of the Hanff household and helped all he could around the house. He planted tomatoes in season in the small backyard near a fig tree he dutifully wrapped in tarpaper for the harsh winter, helped in the kitchen and spent nearly a month putting a fresh coat of paint on the house's interior walls. He had a meager income left over from some investments which were not eradicated and this he chipped in to help with the family expenses.

One of his favorite pastimes was reading from *Plutarch's Lives* and *Tales from Shakespeare* by Charles Lamb. Helene was enthralled, so much so that she preferred Uncle Al to the radio. Her brothers felt differently, but Uncle Al didn't mind a bit. Both Plutarch and Charles Lamb became favorites of Helene throughout her life. Once, as Helene recalled with a broad smile, Uncle Al put some clean laundry in a ball and made a humpback of himself by placing it under his long johns. Thus he became Richard the Third for a full evening, wandering about the parlor with a twisted expression and raging about his "lost horse, Nelly," all to Helene's extreme delight.

The Depression inadvertently allowed Helene's father to refresh his love of the stage. While money may have been coveted, Arthur figured out how to trade shirt samples for tickets to stage shows; box office employees were more than happy to get a good new shirt for four or five back row seats. "We may have been poor," said Helene, "but we saw all the best new shows in town!"

Helene's mother Miriam had a close and dear friend, Jeanette Bron-stein, another New York transplant from the Lower East Side with the "scandalous" reputation of having been divorced from an abusive hus-band back in New York. "Aunt Jeanette", as the children called her, was attractive and "stylish" as Helene remembered her, "with bobbed hair and a bobbed attitude toward life." With only a high school education, Jeanette managed to get hired as a fourth grade teacher at the local school; "with her looks, she could've gotten the job of governor," Helene re-marked. She became a sort of role model for Helene and, as Uncle Al did, read her stories of chivalry and the knights of yore and introduced her to Jane Austen's *Pride and Prejudice*, a book Helene read and re-read through-out her life, one of the few works of fiction she ever enjoyed.

Unfortunately, the surface of life betrayed the undercurrents. One day, when Helene was 15 years old, she returned home early from school with stomach cramps. She entered the house quietly expecting no one to be home. She heard sounds coming from the downstairs parlor and walked in only to discover Jeanette in the arms of her father, "fully clothed but in quite a heated state."

Quick excuses and an awkward cover-up ensued, but the damage was done. Helene's immediate response was to treat the incident as if it had never happened, not revealing the story to anyone at the time and sup-pressing the confusion and distress it caused her. But she was "perma-nently disillusioned" about marriage and family life and she never got over what she felt was the "double treachery" of her father and "Aunt Jeanette." It wasn't until some 40 years later that she finally told her cousin Sharon (Connie) Hanff-Ulrich about the incident, releasing 40 years of suppressed negative emotions that had to have exacted a price. By her own admission, the memory of that day was never far from her mind and probably surfaced subliminally in her relationships with men; she sub-consciously vowed not to be vulnerable and never to "get hurt" by mar-rying. She always referred to men that she dated as "friends" or "dates," never "lovers" or "boyfriends" or any other category that might set her up for the betrayal she experienced that dark day in 1931.

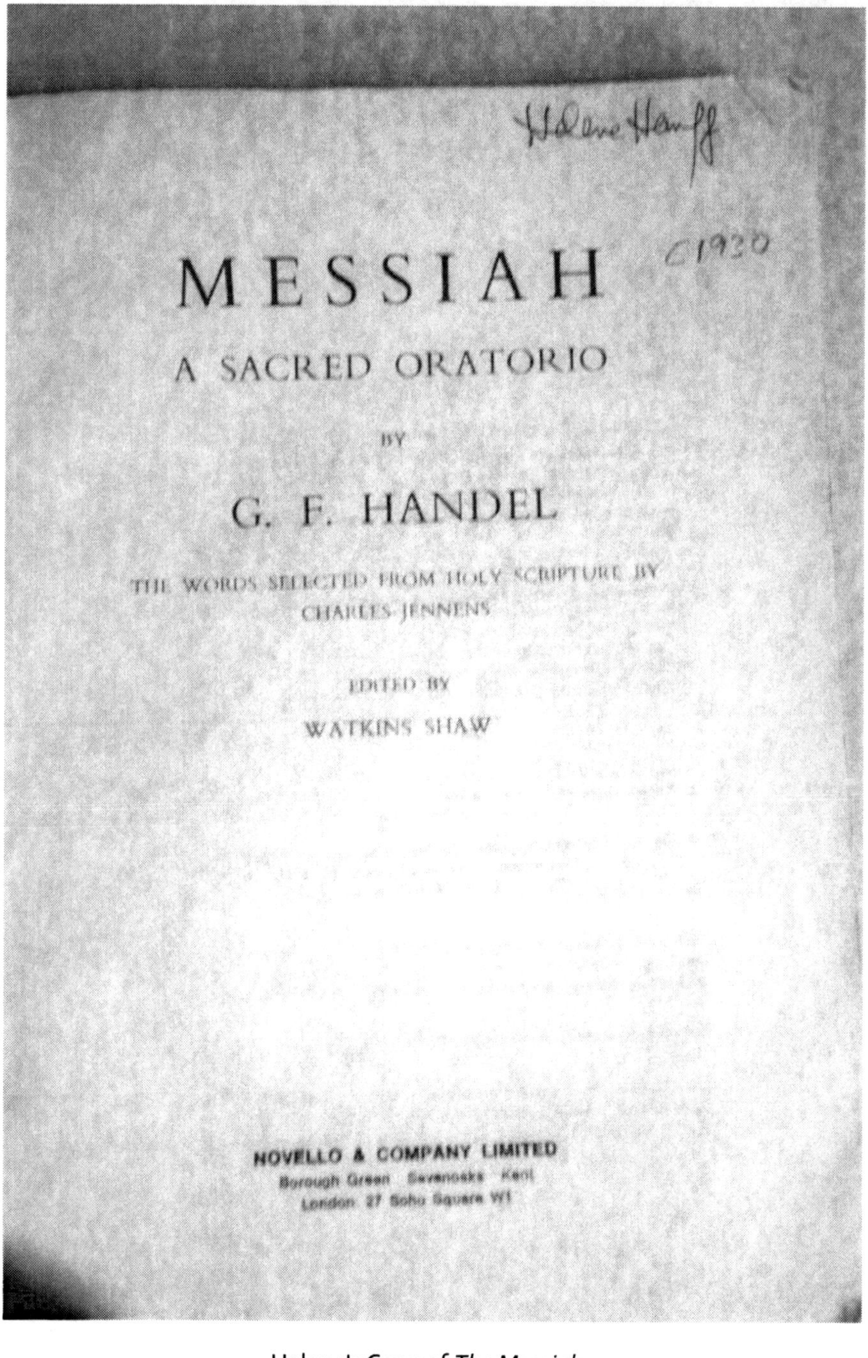

MESSIAH *C1920*

A SACRED ORATORIO

BY

G. F. HANDEL

THE WORDS SELECTED FROM HOLY SCRIPTURE BY
CHARLES JENNENS

EDITED BY

WATKINS SHAW

NOVELLO & COMPANY LIMITED
Borough Green Sevenoaks Kent
London 27 Soho Square W1

Helene's Copy of *The Messiah*

Helene Hanff's High School Photo

CHAPTER 5

SP: One of my favorite stories about you relates to the period when you were a novel reader for a movie studio.

HH: Oh, yeah. In the early 1950s.

SP: *The Lord of the Rings?*

HH: I suppose you read it?

SP: Everyone in college in the 60s read it. Long. Very long.

HH: They handed me this three-volume monstrosity and gave me 24 hours to read it.

SP: That is optimistic.

HH: No. It's a form of torture although I'd rather carry it around for a week than spend an hour reading it. I couldn't even skim it in 24 hours.

SP: But you said it could not be turned into a film.

HH: Anything could be turned into a film. You could read the Manhattan directory and make a movie of it. It had a strange language, 18 million characters and Kodak would have had to open another factory to provide the blank film for it. People would age as they watched it.

SP: It could have been edited down a bit.

HH: Yeah. With a chainsaw.

Helene and her cousin Carolyn grew up together like sisters, remaining emotionally connected throughout their lives. Of all the family, Helene physically resembled Carolyn's mother, Cecile, the most, and was closer to her than she was to her own mother—and indeed, closer than Carolyn herself was to Cecile. The two girls spent a lot of time sleeping over at each other's houses, relishing the freedom they were given by each other's parents— "other people's parents are always easier to be around than your own" Helene reminisced. Carolyn's family had fared better throughout the Depression than Helene's, and they visited England when Carolyn was eleven years old. Already obsessed with the idea of one day traveling to England herself, Helene grilled Carolyn thoroughly for information about the trip on her return. During High School, Helene's English teacher was Helen Bailey, and Helene's love of literature grew from her inspirational teaching. Helen Bailey was later recognized as an outstanding teacher when she was granted the Gimble Award in Philadelphia, which amounted to a stipend of $250 per year for four years.

Helene's cousin, Carolyn, was only three months older. They were extremely close, more like sisters really and they stayed in touch all their lives. Carolyn's "steady boyfriend, "Teddy" who would grow up to be a background singer for a Las Vegas act, tried on several occasions to get dates for Helene.

"I always felt she was more of a fifth wheel, someone removed from the action. Carolyn adored her and so if I wanted Carry, Helene would be part of the deal," he said in an interview in 1993. "It wasn't like nowadays, you know. Getting to first base as they called it then was a major event that required a major effort. I was willing to do whatever it took, but Carry didn't want Helene to be alone. Actually, in looking back, I think now that it was not that at all. Carolyn pitied Helene's awkwardness. Well, I'll be frank, Helene was what we called in those days 'a dog.' She was ungroomed as I recall. One time my friend Bill Grabowski agreed to a blind date with Helene. When he showed up at Helene's, he told me later, she opened the door and he thought, or hoped, he was at the wrong house. Of course, guys were no more sensitive then than now. Our football team had a party we held every year. It was called the 'Bow-Wow Party' and the rules were simple. Everyone contributed five dollars to a betting pool and the bet was this: whoever brought the ugliest date (the Bow-Wow being the 'dog'), won a hundred dollars, which was a ton of money then, let me tell you. Helene had three guys invite her. She went with a guy named Nick Maselli—I think he was a running back, a great looking Italian guy who could have any girl he wanted. Helene was thrilled, as she told Carry, but couldn't figure out what he saw in her. Carry didn't know about the bet, of course, so she said that maybe he wanted an intelligent girl for a change. She went with Nick and girls being sorta dumb when it comes to guys' motives, she didn't notice that all the girls were beasties, some of them so bad, I thought the paint would peel in the restaurant we rented. Anyway, Helene didn't win—or her date, I mean. Nick was pissed. One of the guys brought an American Indian chick that looked like Cochise in drag. Got him a hundred bucks."

Movers and Shakers

CHAPTER 6

SP: Before you wrote *84*, had you visited England?

HH: No. I said so in the book.

SP: So why England? I mean with all the countries in Europe, you picked the one with the worst weather and the worst food.

HH: I didn't pick it to play tennis or to have a three-hour siesta. I love England because of the people.

SP: If you never visited, how could you be so sure about the people?

HH: The literature they produced. The plays. The novels. The poetry. And my people are from there. Not to mention the movies. There's a certain understated elegance that Hollywood never got the hang of.

SP: Have you ever read French or Italian novels?

HH: No. I read some memoirs in translation.

SP: How about French or Italian movies?

HH: I prefer my actors clothed.

SP: So I guess the fact that the British speak English is a good reason to like England.

HH: Are you getting argumentative?

SP: I was born that way.

HH: If you needed to find a bathroom real quick in a foreign country, would you rather spend ten minutes gesturing to someone about what you were looking for or ask 'Where's the nearest loo?'

"Each year, hundreds of stage-struck youngsters arrive in New York to crash the theatre, firmly convinced they're destined to be famous Broadway stars or playwrights. One in a thousand turns out to be Moss Hart. This book is about the other 999. By one of them."

Helene Hanff spent most of her time tucked away in her tiny fourth floor apartment. She had moved to New York in 1936, after a year of college, and had taken up residence in her little corner of the city. She was the definition of a starving artist, trying to make a name for herself as a play-wright. Her skills in creating characters were always given high praise, but her inability to develop a plot proved to be a fatal roadblock with each attempt. She was, however, incapable of quitting.

Each night she would make her way to the second-hand dining table she had acquired from her neighbor, Fred, and write. Sometimes the words would flow, other times it was the gin that would do the flowing. Her parents did not know of her self- proclaimed "rebellious" side, which included a taste for gin and cigarettes.

She viewed a relationship as something that would be a waste of time, stealing away precious moments that could be used for writing. Although that first play that was worthy of being purchased had evaded her, she knew eventually it would happen and she certainly did not want to risk missing that magical moment by being away from the typewriter any more than she had to.

Since she had not sold any plays, she had been forced to find other ways to pay the rent. She was not what people in the acting community considered attractive, so she had failed in landing any roles on stage. Eventually though, she had secured a job in a bookstore a few blocks from her apartment. The owner, Michael, was sympathetic to young artists attempting to make their way in a very difficult world.

The patrons at the bookstore were of every shape, variety, and personality. Helene enjoyed talking with them and using bits and pieces of each of them to develop her characters. She considered this as a little fuel for her imagination. Considering the still raw feeling of the fall of Wall Street, lots of people had a story tell but few ever thought of writing theirs down.

One thing Helene always kept with her was a small pad of paper, in case an idea came to her when she was away from home. She had lots of ideas on her pad, but was always looking for more. Whether she was at work, at her favorite little cafeteria or just walking down the street, Helene was always focused on creating the play that would deliver her to the Great White Way.

Frank Dartmouth, III was a regular at the bookstore. He usually wore a tattered hat and slightly frayed suits. His graying hair would seem to imply that he was in his fifties, but he was actually only in his early forties. He had been a trader on Wall Street until 1929, when everything fell apart. Now, he drank too much, told stories of the '20s, and offered financial advice to anyone who would listen. Helene just called him Frankie.

Frankie was reclined in his normal chair a few feet away from the front counter at the bookstore, rattling on about some stories that Helene had heard several times. She was smiling and nodding occasionally, but her brain was locked firmly into the plot she was constructing on her pad. That was until Michael walked up and slid a sheet of paper in front of her.

She read it quickly and then looked up at him with a smile. He explained that his friend, Gerald Mackley, had asked him to pass these along to anyone who might be interested in submitting a play for a competition he had created. Michael went on to tell that Gerald had inherited a small theater from his aunt. The venue had been closed for almost three years, but he had decided that he would reopen it specifically as a home for up and coming artists. He knew there were hundreds of young writers, designers and actors that would love to get a chance to show off their abilities. So, he was using some of his inheritance to create the Eleanor Mackley Fellowship.

Michael told Helene that he knew she had tried very hard and was certain she could come up with the story that would win her the chance to be a part of the new Mackley Theatre. Helene thanked him and smiled as he walked away. She laid her pencil on the pad and stared at the idea she had been working on. After a few moments, she heard a familiar droning. That was when she looked up and realized that Frankie had never stopped talking. She picked up her pencil, turned to a fresh page and wrote *The Man Who Fell*.

The next two hours were spent writing down everything that Frankie said. She was nearly giddy as she realized that his story was truly interesting. Eventually though, he stood and declared that it was time for him to get something to eat. She asked if she could write his story and he stroked his uneven, dirty beard, as if he were in deep thought. Three painfully long minutes later, he agreed, asking only that he get a free ticket to the show when it hit Broadway. Helene laughed and agreed.

The next two weeks flew by, allowing Helene very little time for sleep and surprisingly she did not even open her bottle of gin. Frankie's story seemed to flow from her fingertips as the pages piled up on her table. It was nearly four in the morning on a Wednesday when she placed the last sheet on the stack and declared the play finished. She felt better about this one than any of the others.

She tied the play together with her typical spool of twine and wrapped it in a page from a newspaper from many months ago. The flyer Michael had given her showed the address of the Mackley Theatre, so she slipped on her coat and severely worn out shoes. She had a feeling no one would be there, but could not handle the idea of sitting at home.

Although it was still before dawn, the streets were quite busy. This was an aspect of New York that she truly loved. It did not matter what time of day it was, there was always something going on. She strolled along past the vacated store fronts, occasionally seeing a baker or shopkeeper who had survived the aftermath of Black Friday getting ready for the day.

Fifteen minutes after leaving her apartment, she arrived in front of the building that bore the address she was looking for. The box office window was covered with plywood and the theater doors were chained shut. Her heart sank as she thought the Fellowship was not real.

As she stared at the cold, dark building, she heard a rustling from a doorway to her left. A man wrapped in a worn out quilt asked her what she was looking for. She had never been one to avoid talking to people, so she told him she was looking for the Mackley Theatre. He told she had found it, but that the new owner had been using the rear entrance. She thanked him, but apologized that she did not have any money to offer him. He told her that okay, but if she ever did have some, he would probably be there.

The sun was just coming up as she walked down a narrow passage along the side of the theater. The shadows seemed to be resisting the light and the alley behind the building was still quite unwelcoming to visitors. Helene looked at the rear of the building, finding a single steel door with a dim light hanging over it. She was about ready to knock when a man approached her from her left.

He asked what she was doing here and she felt uncomfortable for the first time in many months of living in the city. He was a big man with dark hair, wearing overalls, but his face was still obscured by the lack of light. She nervously explained that she simply wanted to find the Mackley Theatre. With that, he stepped into the light and she could see his smile. He told her that he was Gerald Mackley and she sighed with relief as she told him that Michael was her boss.

He unlocked the door and invited her in to see his project. She imagined that the place must be horrible shape, considering what the outside looked like. However, she walked out onto the stage and stared at the amazing theatre. The centuries old wood carvings, stained glass, and beautiful decorations took her breath away. She immediately began dreaming of standing in the wings and watching her play happen on that stage.

Gerald brought her back to reality by asking if the package in her hand was for him. She gave him a broad grin and held it out to him like a first grader hands their straight A report card to their parents. She was only mildly disappointed that he did not rip it open and start reading right then. He did tell her that he appreciated her entry and that he would be making his decision within the month, but that he really needed to get to work as he hoped to have the theater open by the first of the year. She reluctantly left the stage and went back out into the, now well lit, alley.

She tried to fight off the desire to be nervous, knowing it would be a while before she learned if she had won. She had the day off, but decided she should probably try and work every day if she could. Sitting in her apartment would surely drive her crazy. The six block walk to the store, plus a very strong cup of coffee from a street vendor, helped her clear her head as much as possible.

Michael was working the counter when she walked in. She explained that she needed to be working for her sanity and that she had just come from the Mackley Theatre. She told him that he did not even have to pay her for extra shifts, but she needed to be doing something while she waited. He suggested she keep writing, but she told him she did not think she could. *The Man Who Fell* just would not get out of her mind, so writing anything else would be nearly impossible.

He told her to take over the counter and that he would pay her for her time. His only request for some tickets once she won the fellowship. She said she would do what she could, but had no idea if she could ever promise such a thing. He smiled as he walked off toward his office. Helene picked up a worn out looking book from the second hand bin and took her place on the stool behind the counter.

So, it became her routine to pull herself out of bed just after dawn to eat some toast and have a cup of weak coffee. She would then put on some clothes from her sparse wardrobe and head off to the book store. After a minimum of ten hours at work, she would find a bench and watch people for a few hours. Finally, she would go home, have a nice glass of gin, pat her typewriter, and slip into bed to start the routine all over again.

This went on for three weeks and she had settled into the pattern. Day twenty-two was a Thursday and she was quietly walking back to her apartment sipping a cup of hot cocoa. She climbed the familiar stairs but froze as she stepped into the hallway outside her apartment. The cup slipped from her hand as she began to scream with excitement, recognizing the two men outside her apartment as Michael and Gerald.

She raced over and hugged Michael. She realized that she was being a bit presumptuous, so she straightened herself and asked what they were doing there. Gerald laughed and told her that her guess was correct. He had selected *The Man Who Fell* as the winner of the writer fellowship at the Mackley Theatre. She invited them in to her shabby little place, but they happily accepted. She poured three glasses of gin and told Gerald how excited she was to get started. He was impressed by her enthusiasm, which nearly blew the roof off the building when he told her the first show at his theater would be her play. He had intended the submissions to be nothing more than an application, but he was moved by her show.

Gerald explained that the theater would be ready for its first show by the beginning of December and that he would begin work on *The Man Who Fell* immediately. He planned to begin auditions the next week and then on to rehearsals the following week. All this was, of course, dependent on Helene allowing him to use her play. She nearly fell off her chair laughing, as if there was any chance she would not want to see her play performed on a real stage. He placed a contract in front of her. It was simple and the dollar amounts before her left her stunned. She would not necessarily get rich, but she would be just fine for the next few years. She would also be given the title of Assistant Director.

Signing her name seemed surreal, but Helene Hanff was happier at that moment than she had been in a very long time. Gerald tucked away the document, offered up a toast and began explaining the next steps. He had already awarded fellowships for two actors and a director. They were promising and hungry. This was why they agreed to perform without knowing the play.

The trio finished off a full bottle of gin and Michael decided that was a good time to call it an evening. It was very late, but Helene knew she would not be falling asleep anytime soon. She sat at the table and stared at her copy of her contract regarding the play. She thought back over the bleak times that had been her life for the last couple years.

Her parents had not necessarily been a fan of her dreams of becoming a writer and moving to New York. Her father had wanted her to go to college for Accounting and then join him at First Philadelphia Bank. The idea of being a number cruncher for the rest of her life made her want to throw up a little in her mouth. So, after she had won a fellowship with the National Theater as a writer, she packed a few suitcases and left the comforts of home to pursue her dreams.

She had won the right to work on the team for the National Theater's own *Yankee Doodle Beauty*. She read the script after arriving in New York and wondered if she should have stayed in Philly. It was atrocious and she soon found out that the National Theater was well known among writers and actors as a factory for such shows. No one stayed on the National Theater team long, but being able to say you had been through at least one show there looked good on a resume.

Helene had always been shy. Something that was fine for writers, but it had kept her from being very social for the first year in New York. The one person she regretted not getting to know during that time was an actress in *Yankee Doodle Beauty*. Maxine Stevens probably never noticed the homely Jewish girl in the wings as she mixed around with the other actors. She exuded a sense of confidence that made Helene believe she would be a great friend and maybe more. She had never been interested in women in that way, but Maxine seemed to have a way about her that caused things to stir in Helene.

So, when Gerald invited her to sit in on auditions and she saw Maxine walk on stage, she felt like she could not breathe. Gerald did not know what Helene was actually thinking, but patted her on the hand and told her that he thought she was very good, too. That was why he had given Maxine the fellowship for the lead female role. Which, in this case, would be Sarah, Frankie's wife. As soon as the first set of auditions were over, Helene excused herself and slipped back stage. She saw Maxine reading over the script at a table near the soon to be completed green room. Helene gathered herself and walked with heavy feet toward Maxine.

"Hello," Helene said, garnering a smile from Maxine.

"Hi."

"I doubt you know who I am, but I worked on *Yankee Doodle Beauty* at the National Theater with you a few years ago. Anyway, my name is . . .

"Helene Hanff. Yes, I know who you are. And yes, I remember you from the NT. That was a horrible show."

Helene sighed in relief as they chatted about the train wreck of a show they had worked on. The fact that Maxine remembered her made her heart skip a little, but she tried not to show too much excitement. Their session of reminiscing was broken up by the director's call for the next set of auditions. Helene quickly wrote down her address and the address of Michael's book store on a scrap of paper. Maxine promised to visit the book store and Helene rushed back to her seat to watch auditions.

Gerald had scheduled a one-week break between the end of auditions and the beginning of practices to allow his contractor to get some more work done on the theater and to allow the director some time in selecting his cast. Helene had begged Michael to let her work every day that week. He assumed it was because she was nervous about the show, but it was mostly because she did not want to miss Maxine.

Three days came and went with no sign of the actress. Helene walked in around noon on Thursday, expecting nothing different. However, Michael immediately directed her to the reading area. He smiled and told her that a young lady had been waiting for nearly an hour. Helene was in disbelief that anyone would wait for her, but tried to keep herself from running to the small side room at the back of the store.

She rounded the corner and saw Maxine, reading her script. Helene wanted to take a picture. Maxine looked up and simply asked if she could get her autograph. Helene fought the urge to faint. Maxine slipped the script into her bag and explained that she had hoped they could get some lunch before her shift. Helene told her that sounded great and that she was sure Michael would give her some time to go eat.

Michael was happy to stay at the counter for a while, so the two young women were off. They selected a diner two blocks from the book store for lunch, but spent most of the time talking instead of eating. Maxine told her that she was lucky enough to be from New York and that she still lived with her parents on West End Avenue. She was not one to hold back on anything and invited Helene to come over for dinner. Helene accepted without thinking about it.

The afternoon after the lunch was a blur for Helene. Her emotions were being tossed around like sand in a hurricane. She had never had a boyfriend or even a best girlfriend when she was growing up, so she was not sure what this invitation to dinner meant. She only knew that she was going to get to see Maxine again outside of the theater.

The show was set to open in four weeks at the Mackley Theatre. Helene was a nervous wreck and had nothing to quell this since her contribution had already been made. Sure, she was the assistant director, but that was only a title. So, she sat through the practices, trying not to appear nervous. A few people who had gotten a sneak peak gave positive feedback, but she knew the real test would be that opening night crowd. A show could be made or broken in one night. She also knew that she show had to run at least a month for her to get any significant amount of pay from Gerald.

Although she was nervous, she found herself growing quite bored during rehearsals. She decided that she would bring a few of her older plays with her and try to rework them while "watching" the rehearsal. She had been doing this for three days when she was interrupted by someone clearing the throat. Helene looked up to see a frowning Maxine standing a few feet away. They had apparently taken a break, but she had not noticed.

Helene tried to make an excuse, but after a minute or so, Maxine started laughing. She slid into the seat next to Helene and told her that she needed to lighten up. Helene was relieved and then excited as Maxine told her that her mom was expecting a guest for dinner that night. She gladly accepted. For once, she would not be eating dinner alone and she would be enjoying herself all at the same time.

The rest of the day seemed to take forever. Two more rehearsal sessions, lasting until almost half past five, seemed to suck every ounce of energy from the cast. Finally, the director gave up for the day and sent everyone home. Maxine was pulling her hair back into a ponytail when Helene found her just off stage left.

Helene knew it was getting late for dinner and told her she would not be upset if they had to cancel. Maxine just smiled and told her that her parents were not expecting them until at least six thirty. She assured her that everything was just fine as she slipped on her coat. Minutes later, they were talking about anything that was not related to the play as they walked toward West End Avenue.

They made it to Maxine's house at ten after six. Her father, Stan, was in his den smoking a cigar and sipping some brandy. He put down his paper when the girls walked in, making his way over to greet them. Maxine's mother, Joan, emerged from the kitchen looking picture perfect in her powder blue dress and starched, white apron. Helene secretly hoped she would never have to wear an outfit like that. After some quick introductions, Joan slipped back into the kitchen to finish preparing dinner.

Stan led the way back to the den, where he offered the girls a drink. His collection was extensive and Helene was not shy about asking for a nice dry gin. Stan appreciated her taste and poured her a glass as he asked her about *The Man Who Fell.* He explained that he was looking forward to opening night. He had known quite a few people who lost everything due to the stock market crash.

Helene told about her friend, Frankie, from the bookstore. She told how Frankie had been looking for someone to listen to his story for years and she had simply been that willing person. She told Stan that she was very pleased with the cast, but especially with Maxine and Adam Blaine, who would be playing the role of Frankie.

They were all summoned to the dining room at precisely six thirty. A roast, with all the imaginable side dishes was neatly arranged on the table. Helene was not sure if she should eat it or take a picture of it. Stan took his normal seat, then Maxine motioned that Helene should join her on the side of the table to his right. Joan took the seat nearest to the kitchen.

Helene felt truly welcomed by the Stevens family. They enjoyed a wonderful dinner, had a few drinks, and talked well into the night. Eventually, Maxine's parents retired for the evening and left the two girls to chat. Their friendship had reached a new level and they began sharing more information about themselves. Finally, though, Helene decided she should go home, since they would have to be at the theater by eight the next morning.

The streets are never quiet in New York and Helene was not afraid of walking alone at night, since she had grown up in Philadelphia. She always said that Philly was twice as rough as New York. She walked into her apartment and looked around. Her simple little apartment suddenly seemed even lonelier than ever before.

Helene arrived at the theater early the next morning. She had hardly slept and simply wanted to get out of her apartment. Gerald and the director were having a business meeting when she walked in. They paused only briefly, as she willingly walked away. She wanted to see how the box office area was coming along anyway.

Less than an hour later, the actors began arriving and warming up. Helene had taken up residence in the last row, reading over one of her old scripts. For some reason, the projected success of her newest play was giving her confidence to go back and fix some of the others. She was deep in thought, until she heard the day's first rehearsal begin. The voice she had grown to love carried through the theater, as Maxine recited a soliloquy.

Helene watched with joy as her words came to life. Opening day was not very far away and she felt very good about what the audience would be taking in. She tried to stay out of the way, as the last week passed. Maxine was at the theater nearly twenty hours per day and Helene would come and go, slipping in and out without much notice from the others. She liked it that way.

Two days before opening day, she was sitting at the front counter at the bookstore. The little bell on the door gave its familiar jingle, but Helene did not look up. Most of the clientele were regulars and knew where to things were in the store. A slight clearing of the throat by this customer caused Helene to look up. She was greeted by the broad smile of Maxine Stevens. Maxine had a four-hour break, since they were working on a scene that did not include her character. So, she had hoped Helene would be available for a late lunch.

Three minutes later, Kristof, the new guy, had taken over the front counter and the pair was on their way. They discussed a few options, but Maxine finally suggested some deli sandwiches at Helene's apartment. Helene was a little nervous about showing Maxine her terrible apartment, but her friend was quick to tell her she simply wanted to know more about her.

A stop at Kelner's Deli and they made their way to Helene's apartment. She was feeling very anxious, but did her best to hide that as they arrived at her front door. She unlocked the door and pushed it open for her guest. Maxine walked in and took a good look around, immediately telling Helene all the positive things she saw in the place. Helene felt that familiar calm wash over.

The enjoyed their sandwiches, had a couple drinks and talked for a while before going back to the theater. As they approached, the dreary sky above allowed them to notice the flashing lights on the front of the old building. Maxine was about four inches taller than Helene, allowing her to put her arm around Helene's shoulders as they stood for a moment to take in the view. Helene felt a tear roll down her face as she stared at the marquee, which read *The Man Who Fell, a Helene Hanff play, produced by Gerald Mackley.*

Maxine told Helene how proud she was to be a part of this event. A couple of contractors were working on the main entrance and they smiled as they greeted the girls. The younger of the two men suggested they should be the first to try out the new entrance.

Maxine took Helene by the arm and they marched in like conquering heroes. The newly remodeled lobby was gorgeous. Helene could not help but marvel at the beautiful red carpet and the freshly stained wood walls that were original to the building. Maxine pulled her along as they stepped up to the double doors that were the center entrance to the main hall. They smiled at each other as they opened the doors.

Less than forty-eight hours later, a dozen ushers rushed around the lobby. They opened doors and welcomed in surprisingly large crowd. Helene was backstage, trying to keep from vomiting. Her nerves were shot and she could not bear the thought that this crowd might hate her play. Gerald put his hand on her shoulder and tried to assure her that everything was going to be fine.

The director had taken his place off stage right, a personal preference. Gerald did not ask Helene where she wanted to sit. Instead, he took her by the hand and led her out to two seats in the center of the first row.

The seats had been reserved and Helene could not believe she would be sitting amongst the patrons for this.

The curtain was not scheduled to go up for thirty minutes, so Gerald introduced Helene to the couples sitting immediately to their left and right. Calvin and Margaret Winghaven sat to the right, while Julius and Angela Portman sat on their left. Gerald told Helene that these two couples were major investors in the Mackley Theatre and in her play. Both couples were very pleased to meet the young writer and told her how excited they were to get the opportunity to be a part of this.

After those introductions were complete, Helene felt a tap on her shoulder. She turned to see Frankie sitting right behind her. This time though, he was clean cut, smelled and looked sober and was wearing a perfectly pressed tuxedo. He smiled and introduced himself as Frank Dartmouth, III. He thanked her for telling his story, but she assured him that she should be the one giving thanks. She promised to talk to him after the show.

Just before the curtain went up, an usher handed Gerald a small envelope. Gerald opened in and smiled. It was a note from the box office manager telling him the show was sold out. Gerald shared the news with Helene and pulled another envelope from his coat pocket. He told her to wait until she got home to open it, but that it was a little bonus to show his appreciation. He also told her that she was welcome to use the cottage he had inherited in the Catskills. Gerald suggested that perhaps a little break after the show completed its first three-week engagement would be appropriate.

This was all so overwhelming for Helene, but it soon disappeared as the great velvet curtain rose to the ceiling. A proud looking actor in a suit walked across the stage and uttered the first words of the play. Helene could only stare, along with the others, as her first show was under way.

American Geographical Society Pamphlet set

E 35¢

Reader's Digest

ARTICLES OF
LASTING
INTEREST

July 1961

Reader's Digest, 1961

CHAPTER 7

SP: You're well-established as a liberal Democrat.

HH: You sound a lot like McCarthy. Are you now or have ever been a member of the Democrat Party?

SP: Sometimes.

HH: Bailiff! Remove this heathen! Yes. I definitely lean in a leftward direction.

SP: But you really have a love of the British monarchy. Isn't that a little rightward?

HH: They are so grand, how could you not like them? So quintessentially British—it's hard to separate the country from the Queen. It's tradition, a tradition that goes back a thousand years.

SP: So do you think the US of A would do better with a King and Queen?

HH: We tried that with Reagan. It didn't work.

SP: How about the Kennedys and Camelot?

HH: That's below the belt.

Unlocking the door, Helene headed straight into the bathroom and started filling the tub; the pipes ringing out their usual percussion as the hot water rose from the basement of the YWCA. Easing her aching body down onto the side of the bathtub, she removed her shoes, rubbing each foot in hopes of just an ounce of relief. The night's work had been brutal.

It started out simply enough. Helene's boss, Joe Heidt, enlisted her help to get 10,000 copies of a press release out that evening. Helene ran the mimeograph machine until her arm could no longer turn the handle. Then Lois, her colleague and friend, took over as Joe scrambled to arrange the copies into neat piles, ready for distribution. At every opportunity, he glanced over at Helene and smiled, invigorated by her close proximity.

As steam rose from the tub, Helene unrolled each of her silk stockings, laying them carefully across the stool beside the sink. Walking barefoot into the living space, she removed her coat and tossed it casually over the back of the divan. Even though it was nearly dawn, she reached into a cabinet, retrieving a glass and a bottle of gin. As she poured the clear liquid over two ice cubes, a smile spread wearily across her face. A hot bath and a glass of gin. At that moment, life seemed very good to Helene; very good indeed. She toasted her brother's picture before taking a long gulp of gin. Be safe, she thought to herself as she ran her finger across the young man's uniform and rested it, for just a moment, on his lips.

Following her bath, Helene poured another gin and, wrapped only in a towel, laid down on the twin bed in her small, but adequate room. Early morning sunlight left ribbons of light around the edges of the pull-down shade, but, despite the hour, Helene considered nothing other than getting a few hours of much needed rest. She had barely finished her drink and placed it on the bedside table when she drifted off into a dreamless sleep.

At 2:15, a knock on the door startled Helene.

"Miss Hanff. Miss Hanff. You have a telephone call . . . Miss Hanff. Are you in there?" The desk clerk sound slightly unnerved.

"Yes . . . yes, I'm here. I'll be down in just a moment, Marcia." Helene tossed her towel aside and slipped on a pair of panties, buttoning them at the waist. She then secured her bra and pulled a long-sleeved dress over her head. Zipping it, she stepped into a pair of pumps, ran her fingers through her shoulder-length brown hair and headed for the lobby.

"Hello," she said a bit breathlessly into the phone.

"Helene where are you?" Lois asked. "Oh, right, you're at the Y. I called you there, right? Well, anyway, where are you? I mean, you were supposed to be at work two hours ago and Mr. Heidt's kinda steamin'."

"Let him steam," Helene answered. "After what we went through last night, I'm in no hurry to get back there."

"But, he . . . "

"If he wants to fire me, he can fire me. I needed to get some sleep.

There's no crime in that now, is there?"

"Well, no, but . . . "

Interrupting her friend once more, Helene told her she would be there within the hour and hung up. Assuring Marcia everything was fine, she headed back up the stairs to her fourth floor room where she kicked off her brown pumps and reached for another glass of gin. Thinking better of it, she placed the bottle back in the cabinet with a promise to revisit it once the sun went down and she returned home from the theater.

Helene had worked as a girl Friday at the Theater Guild for long enough to experience a string of turkeys. Finally, the buzz was that this next show was going to be a huge hit, despite the abysmal reviews from every other city it played.

"For the next few days, Lois and I were busy on the press release. We had 10,000 copies to mimeograph, fold, seal, stamp and mail . . . on the New York Opening of *Away We Go*. We had about 8,000 mimeographed when Joe came back from Boston and told us we'd have to throw them all away and start over: there had been a title change."

While she had worked for a series of bosses, during her tenure as a Fellow at the Theater Guild there had been two; first being a demanding old maid named Theresa Helburn, who took a promotion just three months after Helene began working there. Even though Helene was considered an 'old maid' herself, she was determined she would not die that way.

"It's such a shame you never married," her aunt would say whenever Helene traveled home from New York to Philadelphia, as though it was unheard of for a woman in her thirties to find love. It was not that Helene never dated. It is just that the men she dated were never the marrying type, so Helene chose not to waste her time with them. She chose rather to spend Saturday evenings curled up on the divan with a newly released novel than out on a date with a boorish companion.

As she was nearing her thirty-third birthday, Helene toyed with the notion of becoming a blonde. Her rationale was that men's eyes would be drawn to her Ginger Rogers-ish golden locks and away from her rather lumpy mid-section. Nevertheless, in the end, she changed her mind. I want a man who wants me for who I am, she told herself, and not because I do a good imitation of someone else. That settled it. By her dateless thirty-fourth birthday, she started questioning that wisdom. Still, her hair remained a mousy brown and her mid-section just seemed to get lumpier.

"Mr. Heidt's taken a shining to you, you know," Lois whispered to her one day at lunch. "He's not a bad catch."

Helene agreed, as she was not at all oblivious to her boss's flirtations. As a young girl, she often dreamt of the glamorous life of a girl Friday who falls in love with her boss and they live happily ever after. But reality was a long way from the fantasy she had created. Not that Joseph Heidt was undesirable. He was six-foot-one, had an only slightly receding hairline, wore a size 38 suit comfortably and held down a stable job. He was actually a good catch. However, as her fantasy presented itself to her, giftwrapped and all, Helene had simply felt nothing.

Unzipping her dress and letting it fall to the floor, Helene stepped over the heap of dark blue fabric and headed into the bathroom. She washed her face, ran a brush through her hair and applied some lipstick to both her lips and cheeks, blotting her thin lips with a square of toilet tissue. Grabbing her slip off the hook on the back of the bathroom door, she pulled it over her head. Next came the silk stockings, which she attached carefully to the garters. She then put her dress back on, stepped into her pumps, wrapped her wool scarf around her neck and grabbed her coat, hat, gloves and purse. Locking the door behind her, she walked down the steps and out into the cold.

"Miss Hanff," her boss chided, "how nice of you to join us."

"Miss me?" she teased, confident he would not be angry with her for long.

"There is work to be done, you know."

"I can't imagine what there could possibly be to do," she replied. "Besides, I don't think my fingers have recovered from the trauma of last night."

It had been a rough night. *Away We Go* was opening in a few days, and despite the bad reviews, the Theater Guild was gearing up for a successful run. Running off 10,000 copies of the press release on the mimeograph machine was bad enough. Then, just as they were wrapping it up for the night, her boss got the news that they had to make a change. Theresa Helburn's office called, saying there had been a title change from *Away We Go to Oklahoma*. Helene's arm ached just at the thought of starting all over again; not to mention her feet, back and shoulders. Joe gave her a feeble smile as he lifted piles of freshly mimeographed releases and carried them out to the trash bins behind the building. Lois followed him, arms weighed down with her own stack of paper, as Helene typed up the revised release, replacing the old title with the new one three times.

As the night began its subtle shift into the early morning hours, the phone rang again. Joe, Lois and Helene looked at each other; their eyes imploring no one pick up the receiver. By this point, all three were not only exhausted, but they were freezing as well, thanks to the economy-minded management who, in an attempt to be frugal, had turned off the heat. Bundled in her coat, hat and gloves, Helene unwrapped the scarf from around her face and answered the phone. Tears formed in her eyes as Joe and Lois listened.

"I see," she said robotically. "Yes, I understand."

Exasperated, she put the receiver into its cradle and relayed the message to the other two.

"Exclamation points. She wants exclamation points."

"Who wants exclamation points?" Lois asked.

"Who else?" Joe answered before Helene had the chance. "Theresa she's-going-to-be-the-death-of-me Helburn wants exclamation points. Where does she want the blasted exclamation points?"

"After Oklahoma. After each and every one of the 30,000 Oklahomas!"

And, so it was. Cold and tired, with stiff fingers and a rising bitterness in their hearts, Helene and Lois sat in the outer office, manually placing three exclamation points on each press release, while Joe called around town, waking up various printing firms and sign painters in a desperate attempt to find someone who could save his hide.

"They're too cheap to heat this place, yet they'll spend thousands of dollars to change the house-boards, playbills, ads, three-sheet posters and souvenir booklets," Joe complained. "And they're gonna have to pay us big time for having to stick around to put these blasted exclamation points after surprise . . . I'll show them a surprise."

What was surprising to Helene was her boss's change in demeanor. She had never seen him quite like this before and, somehow, she found the 'new' Joe Heidt rather appealing. It's just the late hour, she convinced herself. Anyone would look good at this point.

"Miss Hanff? Miss Hanff..." Joe's voice interrupted her thoughts. "Are you with us?"

"Sorry," Helene said sheepishly. "I guess I'm still recovering from last night."

"Aren't we all?" Lois deadpanned.

"Well, snap out of it. We have another long night ahead of us. Miss Taylor, get Miss Hanff a cup of coffee."

Lois looked up at her boss, incredulous that he now had her 'waiting on' her co-worker. "Excuse me?"

"Miss Taylor . . . " The tone in Joe's voice had Lois promptly heading over to the percolator. Helene followed her.

"I'd rather have a gin on the rocks," she whispered.

"Yeah," Lois agreed. "You and me both."

The trio worked until just past midnight, with Joe suggesting they call it quits for the night. Lois was out the door so quickly, they barely had time to say goodbye. Always one to jump on an opportunity, Joe asked Helene if she would like to go to the speakeasy around the corner for a drink. Even though prohibition had been lifted, Joe still patronized a little place that had served him well a decade earlier.

Despite her exhaustion, Helene hesitated. Why not? She reasoned. May as well have Joe pay for my drinks. After the last two days, he owes me.

They ventured out into the cold, which was actually just a few degrees lower than the office they had just stepped out of. With his hand on the small of her back, Joe guided Helene down the block and around the corner to Hal's. The place was much noisier than earlier years, with the jukebox cranking out tunes from the Mills Brothers and men and women crowding the tiny makeshift dance floor.

"What will it be Miss Hanff? Sherry, a nice chardonnay . . . "

"Gin. On the rocks," she interrupted. Sherry? Do I look like a Sherry kind of girl?

She downed the first drink and was about to ask for another when she noticed her boss staring at her, his mouth partly open in an expression of disbelief. Smooth, Helene said to herself. Better slow it down . . . there's nothing particularly attractive about a lush. She smiled at Joe.

"Wow. I didn't realize I was that thirsty," she said in self-defense as she looked at his still full Manhattan sitting on the small round table. A candle flickered between them and she leaned back into her chair, studying her boss. His chiseled features seemed more attractive in the dim light of the bar. The alcohol warmed Helene and she unbuttoned her coat.

"Let me take that for you," Joe said, standing and reaching for it. Helene smoothed the front of her dress, suddenly feeling a bit undressed in front of him. After all, he had only seen her bundled up for the past couple of months as they braved the cold together in the State Theater office.

"You look lovely," he said simply, his compliment flustering her and making her yearn for another glass of gin. Her hair lay flat against her head, having surrendered to the snugness of the hat she had worn for hours. With an attempt at being nonchalant, she tried to brush it behind her ears.

"Let me," Joe said as he reached across the table and gently combed his fingers through the slight waves. "There you go," he whispered as he leaned back to look at her, "absolutely perfect."

"Hey, Joe, who's this looker?" one of the regulars asked him, patting him on the back before turning a chair around and straddling it. "I got one for ya. Did ya hear the one about . . . "

Introducing Helene, Joe gave her an exasperated look, obviously not knowing how to get rid of the joke-telling intruder.

"Listen, Mac, the lady and I need some private time . . . you know what I mean?"

Helene was appalled to see her usually stalwart boss winking at the man. Her hands started fidgeting with the empty glass in front of her as Mac excused himself, once again patting Joe on the back and giving him a "you lucky dog" look. Helene cringed.

After finishing her second drink, Helene told Joe she was calling it a night. While admitting the place was "the bee's knees," she simply had to get some sleep.

"Really, Mr. Heidt, I'm all in," she told him. "Surely you understand."

Accompanying her outside, Joe hailed a cab for her. As she lowered herself into the backseat, he leaned over and kissed her, brushing his lips lightly on her cheek. Helene smiled, despite herself.

Excitement filled the following months. As predicted, *Oklahoma!* was a hit. Joe and Helene attended nearly every performance, rising with the audience at each curtain call. With all the attention he gave her, Helene started to feel, if not beautiful, at least pretty. Her penchant for gin took a hiatus, as she felt tipsy on a daily basis without touching a drop of alcohol.

Even after the nights she and Joe went dancing until the early hours of the morning, Helene woke up refreshed and revived, eager to get to work and see her fairytale prince. Lois just rolled her eyes at the two of them, as they tried to maintain a professional air throughout work hours. Helene moved out of the Y and into a sublet with Lois, a bit closer to the Theater Guild. On the nights she was not with Joe, she would spend hours reading historical biographies and writing lengthy letters to her second cousin, Theo, who was serving in Anzio. Summer was just around the corner and with it came hopes of an end to the war. She missed her brother. With the possibility of a wedding in the not too distant future, she was counting on Theo to be home in time to walk her down the aisle.

After the deaths of their parents, Helene and Theo grew closer than most of the other siblings she knew. They were, after all, the only relatives either of them had, and with Theo being eight years younger than Helene, she felt overly protective of him. The months of missing him after he left for the war, ultimately led her to her affection for gin. That and working for Theresa Helburn.

One night when she and Joe were at Hal's, a drunken patron stumbled over to Joe and said, "So Joey-boy, what are you doing with the dog . . . I mean Bow wow!"

Joe grabbed the guy by the collar, lifting him into the air, and threw a punch that landed the drunk in a heap across the room. Helene just sat there, stunned by Joe's actions, and dazed by what she had just heard. Bow wow? The dog? Her head started spinning. *I am ugly. I'll always be ugly.* She picked up her purse and ran outside; never stopping until she was up the two flights of stairs and safely locked inside her apartment where, at last, she let the tears fall.

The sun cut a path across the living room carpet and settled on Helene's puffy eyes. She opened them slowly and looked around. An empty bottle of gin lay on the floor beside the divan, where Helene apparently spent the night and a better part of the morning. *Bow wow.* She shook her head, immediately regretting it as the pain shot from temple to temple. Standing up tentatively, Helene walked into the bathroom and looked in the mirror at her swollen face and eyes, which were reddened by a combination of tears and alcohol. She winced at the sight of herself and turned away.

Hearing Lois's key in the lock, Helene closed the bathroom door, not quite ready to welcome her roommate home from her weekend away.

"Wowser," Lois exclaimed. "What kind of barnburner went on in here last night?"

Helene emerged from the bathroom. "It was no barnburner . . . just me."

"Not possible . . . no way, Helene. You couldn't have drunk . . . " Lois stopped midsentence when she saw the condition her friend was in. "What the . . . ? What happened to you? I mean, besides the gin. You look awful!"

Translating awful into ugly, Helene went back into the bathroom and slammed the door behind her. Bow wow. Bow wow. The words kept replaying in her mind as she sat on the side of the tub and wept.

A loud knocking on the apartment door made her rush out of the bathroom to try to stop Lois from opening it. She did not want to see Joe. Not now. Not ever.

"I have a telegram for Miss Helene Hanff," the uniformed man said to Lois.

"No!" screamed Helene. "Not Theo. Not Theo."

She collapsed on the floor, crying and refusing to look up at Lois, who was holding the telegram in her shaking hands. When Helene was calm enough, her roommate, who was sitting on the floor next to her, handed her the unopened telegram.

The secretary of war wishes me to express his deepest regret that your brother, Sergeant Theodore S. Hanff, has been reported missing in action since fourteen April over Italy. If further details or other information is received you will be promptly notified.

Uncomfortable and unsure of what to say, Lois said, "Well, at least he isn't dead, right? I mean, it could be a lot worse. You know they're going to find him. From everything you've told me about Theo, he's a resilient guy. He'll make his way home. Why I bet he'll even be home in time for that wedding you're hoping for."

Helene just stared at Lois, as if looking at a stranger. Crumpling the telegraph in her fist, she stood up, walked into her bedroom and closed the door.

The weeks that followed were tough on Helene. She quit her job and stayed in her room most of the day and night, barely speaking to anyone; only leaving the apartment to buy groceries and gin.

One night when her resistance was particularly low, she opened the door and let Joe in. He had been stopping by nightly, gently rapping on the door. Helene would admonish Lois not to let him in and Lois would comply, apologizing to Joe in a low voice.

It was a rainy night in May when Joe finally broke through to Helene. He told her he was in love with her and assured her she did not have to be alone during this difficult time. Gently kissing her on the forehead, he pulled her close into an embrace that tore down the walls in an instant. Shaking with sobs, Helene surrendered to the despair she had been feeling for weeks.

After drying her tears with his handkerchief, Joe dropped down to one knee and asked Helene to be his wife.

"These past few weeks have been agony for me. I don't want to . . . I simply can't . . . live my life without you by my side. Please marry me. Please say you'll be my bride."

Speechless, Helene stared at Joe. As moved as she was by his proposal, all she could think about at that moment was how bad she must have looked. Her hair had not been washed in days and she was wearing a rumpled housecoat two sizes too big.

"Please don't ask me that right now," she said to him. "Let's pretend you didn't just do that."

The look on Joe's face told her she should not have responded that way. He rose to his feet and started toward the door.

"Wait," she pleaded. "You don't understand . . . ."

"I understand plenty, Helene. Good bye."

With the sound of the door closing, Helene once again began to cry. She picked up the photo of her brother and held it to her chest. There were too many changes in her life. Good or bad, Helene was starting to hate change.

She slept fitfully that night, still clutching the picture of Theo. Dreams of airplanes and bombs replayed repeatedly, with Theo's face appearing time and again. The image of him walking her down the aisle stayed with her throughout the next morning, the last image in her dream.

By the time she woke up, Lois had already left for work. They saw each other rarely, as Lois was often out on dates at night and Helene was usually asleep by the time she returned. Straightening up the apartment, Helene got a sudden urge to go back to work. Enough of this pity party, she decided. Maybe Joe will welcome me back to the State Theater.

Finding an appropriate outfit was difficult for Helene, as she had dropped two dress sizes in her weeks of isolation and depression. She settled on a suit of Lois's, hoping she would not mind. Being that Lois was three inches taller than Helene, the skirt was a bit shorter than seemed appropriate, but Helene liked the way it showed off her shapely legs. Bow wow. The thought threatened to undo her. No. I will not listen to you anymore. I am not a dog. Besides, Joseph Helburn is in love with me . . . at least I hope he still is. With that, Helene did one last check of her hair, picked up her handbag and headed out of the apartment.

Arriving at the Theater Guild fifteen minutes later, Helene started to feel butterflies in her stomach. Twice she reached for the doorknob and twice she pulled away. She turned to leave just as Joe opened the door.

"Hell . . . Miss Hanff," he said formally. "What brings you here?" His enthusiasm over seeing her quickly faded into a businesslike demeanor.

"Hello Mr. Helburn. I was hoping to have the chance to speak with you." The awkwardness between them was apparent as he invited her in. Lois looked up from her desk and gasped, not only surprised to find Helene there in the office, but to see her looking so nicely put together after weeks of dishevelment.

"Hello, Lois."

"Helene. It's nice to see you back." Lois replied. "Nice outfit, by the way."

"Oh, this?" Helene curtsied as she answered with a Southern belle drawl. "It's just a little something I threw together."

Following Joe into his office and closing the door, Helene started out by saying she was sorry for the previous evening. Joe brushed it off, obviously not interested in hearing her apology or explanation.

"What can I do for you, Miss Hanff?" Formal and to the point.

His former girl Friday came right out and asked him for her job back. Joe hesitated before answering.

"I'm sorry, but the position has been filled," he told her, still maintaining his professional stance. "But I will be more than happy to write a letter of recommendation for you, Miss Hanff." He stood and walked toward the door. Opening it, he added, "Why don't you stop by tomorrow afternoon and I should have it ready for you. Good day, Miss Hanff."

Helene left without speaking another word to Joe or to Lois. It seemed impossible to her that he would not hire her back. Tears threatened to carry her back to where she had been for weeks, but she fought them, unwilling to submerge herself in misery any longer. She knew what she wanted and nothing was going to stop her from hearing that marriage proposal from Joe Heidt once more. After all, she did not say no exactly. She simply wanted him to propose under different circumstances . . . like under a moonlit sky during a walk in Central Park or something. Not in her dingy sublet with her in an oversized housecoat looking like a total wreck! Why could he not understand that?

A carefully devised plan was needed so Helene could convince Joe to take a risk on her once again. Her first stop had to be the boutique on the corner of 38th and Lexington. Spending most of what was left in her savings on a new wardrobe, one Helene was certain would knock Joe's socks off!

When Lois arrived home from work that night, she asked Helene what she was doing at the office that day. Helene explained she was hoping Joe would let her come back to work, but that he told her he had already hired someone.

"He hasn't hired anyone, Helene. That's a bunch of baloney! We need you back there so bad." Lois leaned closer to her friend. "Do you want me to talk to him for you?"

Surprised that Joe would lie to her, Helene started to doubt if her plan would work. She walked into the kitchen and poured herself a gin, straight up. The two roommates stayed up late into the night plotting a way to not only get Helene her job back, but also to get Joe to propose again . . . this time under the right circumstances. The next day, Lois called in sick.

"You know I need you here today. We're already short staffed. What am I going to do without you, too?" Joe sounded desperate, exactly as Lois and Helene had hoped.

"I'm sorry to put you in this bind, Joe, but I'm running a fever. I doubt I'll be able to make it in the rest of the week." Lois faked a cough. "I think Helene's free today. Do you want me to ask her to fill in for me?"

By the time Lois got off the phone Helene had already spent the better part of an hour getting ready for her return to work. She was prepared to arrive at the office early as Joe had conceded, albeit reluctantly. Dressed in an outfit she was hoping would please him, Helene hugged her 'sick' roommate and set out to win Joe back.

Helene had a perfect cup of coffee in her hand as she entered Joe's office. They exchanged professional and somewhat uncomfortable pleasantries and then set out to accomplish a full day's work. Around noon, Helene casually asked where the new girl Friday was. Forgetting for a moment that he had told her he filled her position; Joe mumbled something about her quitting the previous afternoon. A slight smile crossed her lips, but she turned away before Joe could see it and went out to pick up his lunch at the street side vendor on the corner.

The rest of the week went quickly, with Lois feigning illness and enjoying a few days to sit at home and knit. On Friday night, after a twelve-hour day, Helene asked Joe if he would like to accompany her to Hal's for a drink and a bite to eat. He agreed and they found themselves back on the track to romance once again. Accompanying her to her sublet around midnight, Joe leaned in close. Helene closed her eyes, expecting a kiss. Instead Joe whispered in her ear, "You have your job back, Miss Hanff, if you're still interested. See you Monday." Then he turned and left her standing alone at the door, both disappointed and exhilarated at the same time.

On Monday morning, Helene and Lois resumed their routine of walking to work and spending the day together. It was the evenings that had them going their separate ways—Lois on a date and Helene heading home for a night of reading and dreaming about a future with her boss. After three weeks, however, Helene started wondering if Joe would ever ask her out again.

A knock on the door awakened the roommates on Saturday morning, filling Helene with dread. If they had found Theo's body, she was not ready to hear about it. As long as he was missing, there was still hope that he was alive. She pulled her robe on and opened the door. A deliveryman was standing there with a bouquet of three dozen snow-white roses. The card relayed a simple message. Pick you up at 7. JH

Helene tipped the driver and, after closing the door, began waltzing around the living room with her flowers. Lois walked into the room the two shared a hearty laugh.

At seven o'clock, Helene opened the door and stared at her date. Joe was dressed in a dark suit, with a red rose pinned to his lapel. In his arms was a beautiful bouquet of red roses and on his face was a smile that convinced Helene she had chosen the perfect dress for their date.

Dinner was fabulous, with steak so tender Helene barely had to chew it. In an effort to appear classier than she was, she opted for a nice burgundy with her steak rather than her standard gin on the rocks. Joe seemed impressed.

After dinner, they decided to take a stroll under the full moon in Central Park, holding hands as they walked. And then the moment came. Joe stopped walking and turned Helene toward him. He kissed her softly before resuming the kneeling position that had not worked so well for him a month ago. He was banking on the second time being the charm, because he was certain he would not try for a third time. Helene's eyes danced in the moonlight. This was all she had dreamt of and it was finally happening.

Joe's proposal was sweet and to the point. Helene could not say 'yes' fast enough as she was not letting this opportunity slip away; not this time. They kissed again, but with more urgency than before, making it clear to both of them that this would not be a long engagement. They set the wedding date for late in September, which gave them a few months for the preparations.

As the months passed and the wedding date grew closer, Helene could not seem to shake a depression that was embracing her from within. At first, she did not recognize where it was coming from, but as she started packing a couple of weeks before the wedding and came across the telegram, she then realized what was wrong. She missed her cousin. The thought of her getting married without Theo by her side seemed almost sacrilegious, but there was nothing she could do about it. He was still missing in action and there was no way of knowing when, or if, he would ever be found.

Helene's mother came to mind as she was trying on wedding gowns. She missed her and wanted her advice on which gown to pick. Instead, she had to rely on Lois's opinion and opted for a simple off-the-shoulder satin dress. Very little altering had to be done and after they left the boutique, Lois treated Helene to lunch. Over a couple of bowls of chowder, Helene shared her feelings of loss with Lois, who listened intently to her friend's stories about her parents and her only brother. Lois, in turn, shared some of what she knew with her boss, who was unaware of what had been troubling his fiancée.

Shortly after their conversation, Joe informed Lois he was going out of town for a short trip and asked her to take care of Helene for him. While the trip was secretive, Helene did not seem to wonder about it and used the time while he was away to relax and catch up on her reading.

Another Children's Book

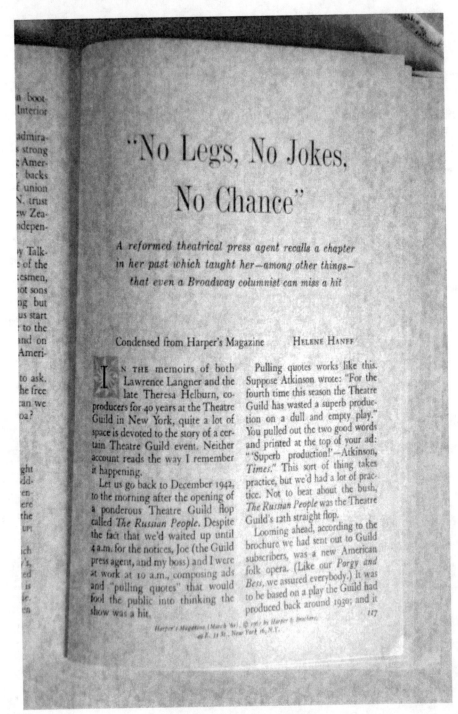

"No Legs, No Jokes, No Chance"

A reformed theatrical press agent recalls a chapter in her past which taught her—among other things—that even a Broadway columnist can miss a hit

Condensed from Harper's Magazine   HELENE HANFF

IN THE memoirs of both Lawrence Langner and the late Theresa Helburn, co-producers for 40 years at the Theatre Guild in New York, quite a lot of space is devoted to the story of a certain Theatre Guild event. Neither account reads the way I remember it happening.

Let us go back to December 1942, to the morning after the opening of a ponderous Theatre Guild flop called *The Russian People*. Despite the fact that we'd waited up until 4 a.m. for the notices, Joe (the Guild press agent, and my boss) and I were at work at 10 a.m., composing ads and "pulling quotes" that would fool the public into thinking the show was a hit.

Pulling quotes works like this. Suppose Atkinson wrote: "For the fourth time this season the Theatre Guild has wasted a superb production on a dull and empty play." You pulled out the two good words and printed at the top of your ad: "'Superb production!'—Atkinson, *Times*." This sort of thing takes practice, but we'd had a lot of practice. Not to beat about the bush, *The Russian People* was the Theatre Guild's 12th straight flop.

Looming ahead, according to the brochure we had sent out to Guild subscribers, was a new American folk opera. (Like our *Porgy and Bess*, we assured everybody.) It was to be based on a play the Guild had produced back around 1930; and it

117

Harper's Magazine (March '61). © 1961 by Harper & Brothers, 49 E. 33 St., New York 16, N.Y.

Reader's Digets article

CHAPTER 8

SP: Did you have any memorable experiences with your fans?

HH: Oh yes. I remember one in particular. A man named Nat_____. He worked in a funeral parlor. He had some stories. But I suppose the most interesting, if you could call it that was a request to do my funeral.

SP: What did you say?

HH: When I'm ready to go, you'll be the first person I call. I think that he forgot that I was Jewish and was expecting an embalming job and a three day wake. Frankly, I don't want to be on display at all. Can't imagine who would.

SP: I would imagine that some day there will be internet websites dedicated to you. How would you feel about that?

HH: Look around. Do you see a computer? No I haven't seen a website of any kind but I've heard about them. I think some of them border on idolatry but I don't mind. I think they're a lot like the old time fan clubs only a little spookier because fan clubs had meetings and you could go to them and meet other people who were gaga over the same person. I went to a Frank Sinatra fan club meeting in Paterson New Jersey once. It was a load of fun. I wasn't much of a fan but I could see why people were so excited about him. It was a social thing. This computer website stuff seems very solitary. I mean you're sitting alone in front of a small screen reading about a person or seeing photos or whatever it is that they put up on it. No talking, no exchange of ideas. I guess it's the new way of doing things and I'm flattered that such a thing could happen but I'm as new-fashioned as a Sears Roebuck catalogue.

SP: I'll say that people do exchange ideas about their "idol" and you can communicate with people all over the world and a good deal of information gets exchanged but it's not exactly a "social event." The meetings are in hyperspace.

HH: Sounds good. I'll make sure I attend the next one.

The stair steps were steep and narrow, wallpapered in a faded rose and green floral pattern, and she had forgotten how tight the passage was up to the storage area in her apartment building. Why hadn't they built this in the basement, she wondered with frustration as she began to breathe a little harder. An attic storage area was absurd and impractical, and she would not miss this part of her apartment building one little bit. She reached the narrow attic door and pushed it open into the dark, cool space. She touched the button on the wall and the lights came on, such as they were, to reveal the two apartment's overflow belongings. Her neighbor below her, Simon, had taken the word storage and given all new meaning to it by seemingly opening the attic door, tossing whatever he had into his space and shutting the door again, all without looking in. Her space was managed quite differently.

They say the attic of one's house represents the brain of one's body, and if this was the case then Helene's brain was in a very organized, predictable state. She saw immediately that her challenge would be not to sort and box up the belongings she had in this attic but instead to reduce the number of boxes to exactly three. Three was a number that worked well for Helene: three the number of unsuccessful plays she had written, the number of men she had love and lost, the number of months she had to find a new place to live, and now the number of boxes she would take away from this absurd attic storage area.

Her few belongings up here might fill three boxes, but she had to look through it all. What had she put up here in the last five years? She bent down and picked up one of the larger bags of paper and headed back for the stairs to her apartment. Going down was much harder than climbing up, of course, because her hands were full and she could not see where she was going. Her foot slipped on the bottom step and she nearly fell as she grabbed for the railing to steady herself. Do not drop this bag all over the floor, Helene thought in frustration, or the contents of the bag will end up directly in the trashcan.

Back in her apartment, Helene put on hot water for a cup of Sanka and placed the bag of papers on the red Formica kitchen table. While waiting for her water to boil, she pulled the contents out of the bag: a copy of her first play, "Winter Love" with the rejection letters carefully paper-clipped to the front cover. The play sat behind a copy of her acceptance letter from New York University; letters from her father in Michigan just before his death; a Playbill from opening night at the St James Theatre of "The King and I." What a wonderful night that was, she thought, she and Raymond were still happy and in love with each other. There were also newspaper articles people had given her on topics about which she could have cared less but kept scattered about her apartment for a few weeks should the sender stop by; pieces of paper with telephones numbers but no names, more paper with addresses but no names, yet others with times and dates but no names. She obviously had kept these small notes in the hopes that names would come to her at a later time.

She poured boiling water into her cup of Sanka, stirred it with one hand as she opened the small refrigerator with the other and drew out a bottle of milk. Cream had risen to the top and opening a fresh bottle of milk was one of Helene's secret pleasures. She scooped a bit of cream for her coffee, recapped and returned the milk to the refrigerator, and closed the heavy door as she walked back to the table, coffee in hand. One by one she went through everything in the bag, tossed things into the trash with little regard to sentimentality, but stopped at the site of Yul Brenner's name on the Playbill. It was a lovely night. She had been seeing Raymond for just a few months, having met him at the public library when they were both looking for a recording of "La Traviata." A coffee around the corner led to a walk through the Village and promises of another meeting the following night. Raymond's smile was broad and welcoming, his manner easy going and relaxed. He had moved to New York City to sing at the Met, and had finally gotten a part in the chorus of "La Traviata." His voice was unheard in the chorus, but when they were alone he sang something from Puccini and she had swooned.

Swooned. What an interesting choice of words, Helene thought, as she looked through the Playbill. How old fashioned and such a perfect description of how she had felt when with Raymond. Not at all herself, suddenly a woman who enjoyed the attachment she had with this baritone voiced, dark eyed man. She swooned in his arms, and in his eyes, and in the laughter of their conversations. She was happy, and had finally let down her guard long enough to let someone in. Her mother was relieved, having assumed that she had raised a daughter so fiercely independent she would never see another generation of Hanff's. And Helene herself was relieved to finally meet a man she could trust and admire and, finally, love. A man who was strong enough not to be threatened by her brains or her ambition or her dry sense of humor.

Helene tossed the Playbill in the trash, and pulled out the other papers in the bag. Old bank statements, a receipt for a man's hat, another for a woolen sweater, a third for rubber rain boots. Why do people keep receipts, she asked aloud. The hat was gone, the sweater was gone,; only the rain boots remained in their place in the hall closet. Why keep receipts for things that are gone? By the time she had emptied the bag, only a small stack of things to keep remained. Her half-drunk coffee was cold, the room chilled, and she rose to turn on the kitchen light. She was struck by the strange space she felt in her heart; this was something she did not ordinarily allow to happen. Looking backwards was a waste of time. Looking forward was a new home and books to read and boxes to pack. Maybe even another play to write. There was a lot to be done. The idea of walking back into the attic was simply too frustrating to face, so instead she walked to the front door, put on her jacket and loafers and left for a walk in the rush of people on the streets, known as New Yorkers.

"What are you doing for dinner?" Simon asked as he approached her in front of their building after her brisk walk.

"Nothing yet, I have not even thought about dinner," Helene said and without stopping continued, "Have you seen those new damned signs on the corner of Bleeker and 4th? Can you believe they have put up a sign that tells us when to walk and not walk across the street? Like anyone in this city who walks needs to be told how to cross the street. Next thing they'll do is give us tickets if we walk when we shouldn't. Why do people keep changing our city, Simon?"

"I just saw one around the corner. Are they going up everywhere, or just certain corners? I bet they are testing them, watching to see how many people get flattened paying attention to the sign and not the cabbie turning left on red. Anyway, I want Chinese food. Let's walk down to Yen's and pick up some food. Ernie Kovacs is on the television tonight. Have you seen him yet? He is fantastic. Dancing forks, singing toasters, and that moustache of his! You have got to see this show!"

Helene stared at him, bemused. Television? She did not own one of the things, they were invasive and just another example of a modern day reason to stop reading. That, and she probably could not get her work produced on television either, so why bother. But she liked Simon, and liked spending time with him. From a small town in Pennsylvania, Simon had come to New York in search of a life filled with books, readers who read them, and writers who write them. Dreaming of owning a bookstore one day, he managed to begin working at the Mulberry Street Library in Soho by volunteering to shelve books. Slowly he had worked his way up to assistant librarian and all of the responsibility that job brought with it. Simon had friends but Helene had met very few of them through the years. Now they would be moving and no longer neighbors. She would miss his company.

They walked to the restaurant which smelled so good they decided to sit and have dinner. They ordered, agreeing to share dishes, and each had a cold beer. Simon talked about work, his frustration with the card catalogues and color coding, where he was going for the weekend, and whether she had seen the photo on the cover of Life this week. Working at the library had many perks, but for Simon one of the best ones was the endless infiltration of magazines. Imagining over a hundred magazine subscriptions coming to her home each month, Helene shuddered. But Simon loved them all, from *Guns and Ammo* to *National Geographic* to the new *Mad Magazine.*

"Simon, I had another play rejected last week," Helene said suddenly, "and I feel so defeated."

"What was this one about?"

"Couple in love, couple fighting, couple learn something new, couple make up. I thought I really had something this time, I really did."

"Helene, when are you going to write about something you care about? You couldn't care less about couples and love and fighting. You are more about passion and beliefs and struggles. All of that with humor, by the way."

She thought about what he said for only a moment and replied, "I write what I think will sell. Love and sentimentality sell—"

Simon interrupted and said, "Westerns sell, too, but I don't see you writing *High Noon*."

"I'm not a western sort of girl, you're right. I write about spring in New York, that time of possibilities and optimism and love because that is what people are buying. I know that is what they are buying. Do you know what book I just passed over to my boss? Two people, both professional, both interesting, sharing a party line. They meet on the party line, argue over the party line, and eventually fall in love despite the party line. That is what sells. It's going to make a great movie. Do I want to write that kind of stuff? No, but Mr. Rouse and Mr. Green are going to have a hit movie on their resume in a few years. It might as well be me."

"You are more intense than that and it's why you just won't sell it. People who can write that kind of story believe in that kind of story. You should be writing a play about Joe McCarthy or the failure of the Nuremberg trials to repair the damage done by the Nazis. You should be writing about a woman who fights convention and becomes a dedicated defender of women or something. Something worthy of you."

Helene smiled at him and him and said, "Simon, you remain my biggest fan. You also credit me with much more fire than I have. But I will think about what you've said. And I'll give you the one that just got canned and you can tell me what you honestly think of it. OK?" Helene finished off the beer in her glass, signaled the waiter for the check, and continued picking at the chow mien. She was tired and wanted to go home, sit in a hot tub and begin reading the manuscript she brought home from work. Work was one of the things in life she enjoyed. Work, and a hot bath.

When they left the restaurant, wind met them squarely in the chest and they pushed slightly as they went out onto the street. How was it that so much could be happening in a person's life, Helene began thinking, and still a person felt so little. I need inspiration, and tucked her arm in Simon's as they walked down Greenwich Avenue inspiration and a new place to live.

"Simon," she said to his profile, her dark hair prickling her cheek when she turned to him, "How are you doing looking for a new apartment?"

"I don't want to move. I figure if I just stay there, they can tear it down around me."

"Really, hmm. Have you found anything? I looked at a place yesterday. They wanted a hundred dollars a month and the whole place was the size of my kitchen now. For that money, I want a separate bedroom."

"I found a building off Cooper Square on Varrik I think I like. They have three flats available. Want to move in there with me?"

"Can we go see it tomorrow? Maybe I need a change of scenery to write something great."

They were in front of the building and Helene said, "I love this building, I really do. I hate to see it go." She loved the solid stone, the thick, steep steps creating the familiar welcome, the leaded glass of the front door. She loved the smell of pot roast when she entered the front hall. She loved the narrow stairs leading to her apartment when she wasn't carrying large bags. She loved the view from her apartment, the city, people walking, cars humming and occasionally giving their raucous honks. For fifteen years this had been home. Soon it would be a Rexall, or a high rise.

Helene entered her apartment, slid out of her loafers and hung her jacket on the coat tree. In the kitchen she took out a crystal wine glass from the cabinet and poured herself a glass of wine. As she turned on the light in her bedroom, she stopped and stared in her mirror above her dressing table. What was this flatness, this slight discontent? Her job was going well lately, and the books she was assigned to read better than those in the previous few months. This was not the first play to be rejected; surprise and shock were no longer attached to failure. She was long over the heartbreak of Raymond, had forgotten the exact color of his eyes, the exact scent of his aftershave. Having accepted the fact that she would never again let herself love someone the way she loved him, she had also accepted this life of reassigned passion.

Who did she see in the mirror? Her head turned slightly as she assessed the woman staring at her: when was the last time she had her hair styled or colored? The lines in her face had established permanence, the dark circles beneath her blue eyes undeniable. Helene stared, expressionless, into the mirror with the ceiling light reflected in its glass and wondered if 'plain' would be a description: "Helene was a plain woman, unadorned by paint and jewels." Would 'unattractive' be more accurate: "Despite her attempts at hiding it, Helene was a rather unattractive women, mouth a little too large for much lipstick, eyes a little too small for dark eyeliner, and dark brown hair unruly and slightly grey." Nondescript, neither stunning nor frightful, with no remarkable characteristics to set her apart from millions of other plain women. There was a time when this summation would have reduced her to tears. At middle age, it simply sat there like fact, leaden and factual and unremarkable. She sipped her wine and continued to stare into the mirror.

No matter how she viewed herself in the mirror, it was definitely time to do something with her hair. She remembered once in grade school the boy she liked was more interested in a girl with blonde hair. Helene went home that afternoon and, while her mother entertained the bridge ladies with sherry and cigarettes, found the bottle of peroxide under her bathroom sink and, with the concentration available only to the jealous, yearning young, poured the contents onto her head. She sat with her mother's Forefeet hair dryer and baked the peroxide into her hair. Fifteen minutes later, she looked into the mirror and screamed. Lillian the housekeeper ran into the bathroom seconds later. They both looked wordlessly in the mirror at Helene's new orange hair. Later, as she sat in the beautician's chair and the consultation began between her chain smoking mother and the robustly large stylist about remedies for this seemingly life-threatening situation, Helene looked intensely at her reflection and wondered if any boy was worth all of this. Let Carol with the beautiful blonde hair have him. She'd never change anything about herself for a boy, never again.

Despite the memory, the reality of her hair was it needed a good cut, simple styling, and a long sit under the hair dryer. Tomorrow she would call for an appointment. No matter what she did with her hair, however, Helene knew she would always look the same, thin and tired and a mile short of pretty. But there was something else there, something about that women in the mirror Helene could not identify. She drank the last of her wine, and began to turn away from the mirror when she stopped. Looking just a moment longer, she whispered "passionless," then turned to draw a hot bath and read.

When she woke in the morning, the sky was clear blue, the air from the open window crisp and cool to the touch, and she stayed in bed just a moment more to breathe in the cool air. What was today? Wednesday. Manuscripts to finish reading, hair appointment to make, lunch with a writer whose work was recently accepted by Simon and Schuster, then afternoon meeting with her boss to discuss the party line book and its possibilities. It was a full day, a good day.

But as she walked to work that morning, the city humming with people rushing to work, cars rushing to get people to work, busses moving faster than usually shuffling people to work, Helene felt oddly discontented. Why? She could not put her finger on it. Was it the move, about which she had done nothing other than sort through one bag of papers from the attic? Was it her job, endlessly reading writers who had successfully published their works while she had not? Was it the lack of a man in her life? Helene thought she had reconciled all of this a long time ago: life was better working, having casual affairs with men of non-threatening substance, and writing.

Writing. Was it her writing? She stopped at the corner and stared at amazement at the flashing sign: Don't Walk, Don't Walk, Don't Walk. Whose absurd idea was this? Had Impellitteri lost his mind? Had we come to the point where we cannot judge whether or not to cross a street? Had everyone around her lost their minds, standing at the corner waiting to be told when to cross? Were we all turning into lemmings? Her outrage was palpable as she walked down Bleeker to her office. Maybe in Detroit, or Philadelphia, but New Yorkers were not going to stand for this. A letter to the editor was in order, and Helene was composing the letter in her head as she walked into her office building through the revolving door.

The call came in the early afternoon. Helene grabbed her jacket and her bag and ran out into the street, hailed a cab, and got to Columbia Presbyterian Hospital all within thirty minutes. Thank God I don't have to do this on a regular basis, she mumbled as she flew into the emergency area.

"My mother, Miriam Hanff, was just brought in by ambulance; can you tell me where she is?"

The woman looked at the list in front of her and said "Hanff, Hanff—I don't see a Hanff here, dear, go down the hall and to your left and see if the ER nurse can tell you anything."

Helene ran down the hall and stopped at the nursing station.

"Your mother is fine, she was hit by a car," the crisp white uniformed woman said, "but she is going to be fine. Would you like to see her?"

The two women walked around a set of chairs and down the corridor to a curtain which the nurse drew back to reveal Helene's mother Miriam. She was resting, eyes closed, and Helene heaved a sob of relief and exhaustion and deep sadness. Miriam's eyes opened and she smiled.

"Well, here I am, just the way they love me, in bed with my hair a mess!" She motioned to Helene to come sit with her, and moments later her mother was explaining what happened.

"I was at the corner of Broadway and 81st and was in the middle of conversation with Sarah—did you see Sarah outside? She was roughed up a bit in the fall, skinned knees and hands, but I think she's okay. Anyway, we were talking about that book, you know the one? Oh, damn. Oh, *The Invisible Man* that Ralph Ellison wrote. Have you read Malamud's *The Natural* yet?" What a good movie that would make! Some book! Make sure it is in your pile to read, dear.

"Anyway, so we were talking about this book by Ralph Ellison, Sarah and I, and—did you know that Sarah is not seeing Jonathan any more? It is—"

"Mom, the accident? The car that hit you?"

"Oh, yes, well we were talking and walking and I was half way across the street when a car honked its horn and the driver screamed at me "lady, look at the sign!" and I looked up to where he was pointing and there is an electric sign on the post telling me "Don't Walk." Well for crying out loud, who ever heard of a sign that says "Don't Walk?" I sure did not see it, and even if I had I would have walked if I damned well wanted to. This is all so absurd, telling people how to do this and when to do that; the government is becoming so—"

"Mom!" Helene almost yelled, and the nurse looked over from her station to see what was happening so Helene turned back to her mother and said "Please tell me what happened. Did the car knock you down? Did the driver go get help? What happened?"

"Oh, yes. Ok, so he pointed at the sign and while I am looking and opening my mouth to tell him what I thought he could do with the sign, a car came up behind him and hit him. He deserved to be hit, stopping in the middle of the street to tell me when to walk. Anyway, when the car hit him, he lurched forward and the car slammed into me and knocked me down. Sarah fell down too, but she did not hit her head. I hit my head."

Helene took her mother's hand and sat quietly, letting things sink in. Her mother closed her eyes and whispered "God I want a cigarette." Helene saw her at her dressing table, her hair straight and black, her make-up so theatrical and extreme that it worked for her, her nails painted blood red, one hand holding the cigarette holder, the other a gin and tonic. This woman, as unconventional and absurd as they come, was her mother. The bond between them, sometimes strained, unbreakable.

"You look so unhappy, dear. Has this upset you? It's nothing." Her mother's voice was unusually soft and sweet, like a hand brushing across her cheek, Helene thought.

"Well, rushing to Columbia Presbyterian to find your mother has been hit by a car does not do much for the spirits." Miriam rolled her eyes at her daughter and they both smiled slightly. "My play was rejected again today by yet another producer. I am bereft, cannot find my way suddenly. I thought this play was a good one. You liked it, I liked it, funny and cute and just what people are going to see now. *The Seven Year Itch* made it, *Peter Pan* was a huge—"

"Helene, so were *A Streetcar Named Desire* and *The Children's Hour*. And you know what the difference is? Lillian Hellman writes about her passions, her beliefs, her soul. Tennessee Williams nearly dies from the power of his own passion. Life is short, my dear. One day you are living and the next day you are hit by a car and dead. No sense in saving yourself for the afterlife. Write about what moves you, what sends you to the edge, what means more to you than anything else. Write because it is inside of you crying to be released, not because it will sell somewhere. It may never sell anywhere, but until you write without caring you will never really write.

"Now, leave," her mother said and closed her eyes, "I am an old woman who has been hit by an idiot reading a "Don't Walk" sign. Go home and live, Helene. Live as if you only have the minute at hand to do so. Write about what matters in the minute you have to live. And don't waste your time. Oh, and get me a cigarette on your way out. I have no idea what happened to my holder. Damn, that was a beautiful one, ivory."

Helene kissed her mother's cheek and gently rubbed hers against it. That woman is as strong as an ox, she thought, and got away with this one. Those signs, those signs! What are people thinking?

Helene used the pay phone in the waiting room and called work to explained she would not be in that day or the next in order to be with her mother. The sky was dusky grey-blue when she walked outside, the air sweet and familiar. She began walking back to her apartment, faintly aware of the New York bustle around her, and decided instead to hail a cab. Was that it she thought as she sat back and stared through the window? Had she lost her passion when Raymond left her? Had she gotten stuck and bored and mindless? Tired, she just wanted to be home.

Simon was outside sitting on the stoop of their building. He smiled when she approached and asked "Do you want to go look at that apartment?" She nodded and they walked together the few blocks to the similar-looking building in the middle of the block. An old man answered the buzzer and let them in.

"Which one of you wants the apartment?" the old man said, frowning. "No funny business in here."

"No, we each need an apartment," Simon replied. "We live a few blocks away, the block that is being torn down. Can we see what you have?"

Helene smiled at him as they followed the old man up the stairs. The building smelled of pot roast and brown bread. Life was going to get better.

When she got home, she told Simon she needed silence and a symphony, and they parted ways in the staircase.

"Thanks, Simon. It's a great place at a great price, and I would never have found a place on my own. I would have put it off until the very last minute. I really appreciate it." She tilted her head up and kissed him on the cheek. "See you soon. Start collecting boxes!"

Her apartment was quiet and peaceful, and Helene slipped out of her coat and shoes. With a glass of wine in hand, she called the hospital to check on her mother who was, of course fine and entertaining everyone with her stories of her marriage to the Count. She sent her love, hung up, and walked slowly into the bedroom. Her typewriter sat covered under its plastic case. Helene walked around the room and thought about writing. What did she want to say? Did she want to speak of love, of death, of conviction? Who was this woman inside her plainness calling to her? Would she be up to the challenge of giving her voice?

The cover removed, Helene slid a piece of paper into the carriage and turned the end knob. The paper clicked into place, and she sat down in front of the machine. She placed her fingers on the keys in perfect position and waited. Her mother's words whispered into her breath and into her fingers and she began:

Scene: Hearing Chambers, House on Un-American Activities Committee, Joe McCarthy sits on the dais shuffling papers...

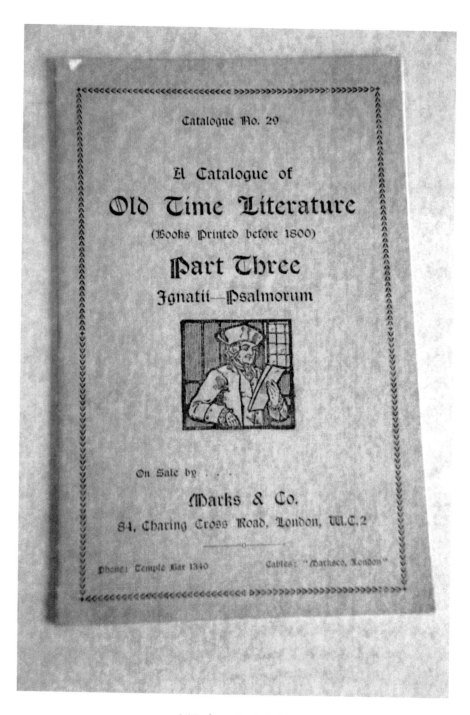

A Marks & Co. Catalogue

Helene's first book

CHAPTER 9

SP: On the basis of your recommendations, I've read a few chapters of some of Arthur Quiller-Couch's books. They're better than sleeping pills.

HH: Very funny. I couldn't afford the tuition to a fancy liberal arts college like someone else in this room so I did the next best thing: I got some books that had lectures on English literature. I learned a lot from old Q, I can assure you.

SP: I don't doubt it. Actually, I'm patronizing you. I do doubt it. That guy was about as progressive as Pope Leo X. Stodgy would be a compliment. I think there's a difference between appreciating literature from another age and reading lectures about that literature from a guy who probably thought Oscar Wilde should have been imprisoned. His views are a little less than enlightening.

HH: I'm an old-fashioned person. What can I say? I think he knew his stuff and he conveyed it to me. Next topic, Mr. Know-it-all.

With success as a playwright still eluding her, Helene Hanff found a job in 1948 as a reader for a Warner Brothers, one of approximately forty they had on staff at any one time. She had to pick up a novel or a screenplay from the studio offices at 4pm, take it home, read it, write a synopsis and return the manuscript to the studio at four the following day. She was paid $6 per synopsis, a figure which eventually rose to $10.

After fifteen years in New York, Helene had still not been able to sell any of her plays. She worked for a period for Irving Caesar (author of *No, No, Nanette*) writing press presentations for his new musical *My Dear Public*, but had no more success selling Caesar's work than her own.

Still working as a reader, she was spotted by a story editor for Warner Brothers, Jacob Wilk, who moonlighted as a theatrical producer. Wilk believed she should write a script for Broadway. He tried to sell a play by her to every producer in New York (including Leland Hayward, who was out of the country on his honeymoon, and Irene Selznick, who was in the hospital with a minor heart condition). He persuaded Helene to rewrite it twice but still could not find anyone to produce it.

She returned to her life as a reader. In 1952, Helene Hanff was offered her first paid scriptwriting job. Jacob Wilk's assistant Gene Burr had left Warner Brothers for television and on Wilk's recommendation offered her work for a new series, *The Adventures of Ellery Queen*. "I was always very scornful of television," she said, "and I only took the job because I had to have major dental work which cost $2,500."

In 1953, while she continued to work as a reader for the next five years, she related her horror when asked to write a synopsis of J. R. R. Tolkien's *The Lord of the Rings*. "I read the opening sentence of the first volume and phoned around several friends to say goodbye, because suicide seemed so obviously preferable to 500 more pages of the same." When she handed in her invoice for reading the three volumes she added an extra $40 for "mental torture". According to Helene, they paid it.

The Adventures of Ellery Queen paid for the teeth but did not extend to financing a proposed trip to London to visit Frank Doel. "In a way I wasn't too upset to cancel my trip to England," she said later. "I was wary of meeting Frank, I had a feeling we might disappoint each other, that it would fatally interfere with our correspondence."

Meanwhile she became what she described as "*Ellery Queen's* special writer of arty murders", and wrote plots about a murder at an art gallery, one at the opera, two at the ballet and one at a Shakespeare festival. "We were just getting round to murder at a rare book shop when they took the show off the air."

R. Dick Archer, her immediate superior at the production company for Ellery Queen said, "We could always count on Hanff for writing something that would offend no one. She did this effortlessly because she really never did look beneath the surface of anything. She was the real 'cock-eyed optimist' who thought everyone was good at heart or had good and decent motives. I imagine that if she had written about Adolf Hitler, she would have made him out to be just another guy who was misunderstood and that underneath it all, he was just a poor boy trying to make a living. Believe me, I thought of just such an assignment as a joke. If there was someone who had no idea about people, it was Helene. She really believed most of what she read in history books and took it at face value, even if those books were written for fifth graders. This superficial approach to everyone and everything made her a perfect fit for television because television was aimed at idiots or, more accurately, the American viewing public which knew about as much about politics or history as a gopher on gopher prairie. My guess is that she would enjoy reading about John Donne as much as she would about Howdy Doody. It was all good, like the world, and if Josef Stalin was killing twenty million people or the Americans were molly-coddling Nazi war criminals for military secrets, then Helene thought that was just fine because we are all just fine. At times I thought she was a simpleton, but it wasn't my job to criticize or judge as long as the work product was soft sell, easy to understand and pap for the brain."

In December, 1953 she began work on Hallmark Hall of Fame, a television program devoted to dramatizing the lives of "great characters in history" with a sugary coating, something Helene felt particularly able to do. After all, she constantly romanticized the lives of writers, especially people like John Donne and William Hazlitt. She distinguished herself during her time with Hallmark by devoting an entire script to the Greek slave girl Rhodope (whom she believed had told Aesop his fables). On the morning of transmission, she read a review of a new book on brothels and discovered that Rhodope was one of the most famous prostitutes of the ancient world. Aided by the staff of the television station, she concealed the fact from the show's sponsor, Joyce Hall, who insisted his programs should always have a high moral tone. "The show was the last one I needed to do to pay for my teeth, so I was determined to get it on the air at any cost." It was broadcast as planned and the station received only two letters, both praising it for "the interesting way in which it explored history".

After working for Hallmark, Helen Hanff transferred to the Matinee

Theatre, where she became the principal scriptwriter, responsible for producing an hour-long program every month (actually forty-two minutes, considering time for commercials). This was followed by a year of freelance writing paid for by a grant from CBS television under a grant from Walter Annenberg. Her job was to produce a dramatization of America's history lasting two hours (again, allowing for commercials). The program was never aired and Hanff returned to popular television with a period as a writer for Playhouse 90, a series of 90-minute plays with contemporary themes.

By the late 1950s most television companies left New York for Hollywood. Helene was unwilling to leave her home in Manhattan; she felt she was unsuited for a life in California as she had never learned to drive. "Playhouse 90 was replaced by a game show, and I was unemployed again."

By 1960 she had stopped writing plays for both the theatre and television and began to concentrate on magazines as a source of income. She wrote for Harpers Bazaar and the New Yorker before being asked to write her autobiography. Underfoot in Show Business was published in 1961 and she followed it with two more books, an account of her devotion to Sir Arthur Quiller-Couch (Q's Legacy) and then in 1970 84 Charing Cross Road. In New York, she spent her time researching a walking guide to the city entitled Apple of My Eye, which was published in 1976. On the radio she became a monthly contributor of accounts of life in New York to Women's Hour on the BBC from 1978 to 1985.

By the late 1980s, after the enormous success of 84 Charing Cross Road, Helene, then in her early seventies, began to reduce the amount of work she produced. She was diagnosed as suffering from diabetes in 1989 but continued to smoke and drink, although both were prohibited by her doctor. "I gave up sugar, but that was easy because it gave me cramps in my legs. That's my advice for all you diabetics out there, stay off sugar."

In 1992 Helene Hanff published her last book, A Letter from New York, a collection of her earlier Women's Hour talks. She continued to live in the same apartment she had leased in the 1950s on the strength of her scriptwriting contract and she continued to read English poetry and to visit England as often as possible. "If I had a million pounds and my life over again," she said, "I'd have a flat in Marylebone and spend my days walking around London looking for Noel Coward's Mayfair, Samuel Pepys's Fleet Street and Isaac Walton's meandering river."

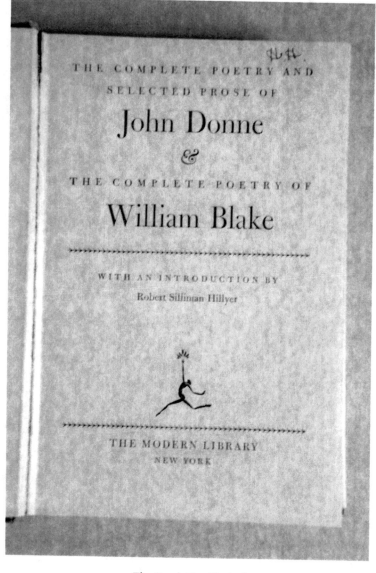

The Book She Hurled

A Hanff textbook

CHAPTER 10

SP: I notice that you rarely write about books written by women.

HH: Good observation, I guess. I never noticed it.

SP: Can you explain that?

HH: Well, women were not accepted as writers until the Victorians and even then, it was considered not very lady-like.

SP: I know how much you like Jane Austen's work.

HH: True. She was not an earth-shattering type of writer. No observations on deep issues and all that sort of thing.

SP: So what appealed to you about her?

HH: Well, like the 20 billion other people that enjoy her novels, she was a good story teller. No angst, no trembling before an unforgiving universe. Just a nice chat over tea about how cute Mr. Darcy was. I wish I could say the same for you.

SP: Ouch.

Maybe it was loneliness that drove Helene to spend her evenings at the Democratic Club in Lenox Hill. She told herself it was idealism.

The country was being swept in the 1960s by the winds of change. For someone who had grown up with the century, the waves of new thinking that were spreading over the country were exhilarating and reminded her of when she was a girl. Women's lib—why, that had started way back when she was a teenager in the 1930s. She remembered how the flappers had seemed to her as a young girl. She had admired their red bee-stung lips, their cigarette holders and the careless way they held them, their short skirts and bobbed hair, and their unrestrained movements to jazz strains. In contrast to most women of the time, who were still wearing corsets, heavily-laced shoes, and who wound their never-cut hair into elaborate whorls and twists on their heads (held by a million hairpins) the flappers had seemed the epitome of freedom to her.

She saw their modern counterparts in that generation's grand-daughters, who went without bras, left their hair to grow where it would, who listened to music with wild guitar riffs and bass so heavy it gave one headaches. She liked them, these earnest, liberated New Left women, and they were some of her best canvassers.

Having been elected the Democratic Club's first woman president, she was in charge of getting out the vote and drumming up the dollars, something she proved to be extremely good at. Lenox Hill and the whole Upper East Side were some of the best political fundraising territory in the country, so her branch was extremely successful.

She was known as unbending, utterly devoted to the cause, and expecting others to be equally so. No one suspected how lonely she was. No one knew how she spent holidays fretting away in her apartment, waiting for the next meeting at the Democratic Club, waiting for the time to pass until she could be with people again. She had no relatives nearby and no friends. She told everyone holidays were a welcome respite from constantly being with people and that she fully intended to relish her time alone. They believed her because her irascible nature made them believe she did need a break from everyone else's incompetence. Yet she spent holidays gazing out the windows of her apartment, watching passersby and wondering what it would be like to be going to a holiday dinner—in a Norman Rockwell-type setting—full of warmth and the laughter of children. She had never believed in Norman Rockwell's America—but the thought of being invited to such a dinner made a tear drip down her face, which she hastily wiped away. She couldn't deny that going to meetings in the evenings and on Sundays took the edge off of loneliness.

Things had never worked out well with men. She'd had relationships—even a short-lived engagement. She was too much of an individualist to adjust to someone else's beck and call. Plus, she liked to work, and most men of the decades when she was young expected a wife to stay home, take care of the home, and raise the children. She wanted to work, to prove herself.

Yet even her work was isolating and added to her loneliness. She was a free-lance writer, and contacts with people were limited to tight-lipped

Stephen R. Pastore

conversations with editors about assignments and dropping off her work
to revolving secretaries who probably made more money than she did.

She liked her life. She just wished there were more people in it.

One Thanksgiving evening, when she realized the whole country was
probably sitting back and watching football, comatose with food, she decided to go for a walk. She had cooked a turkey for herself and made potatoes and gravy, opened a can of cranberry sauce, and drunk a glass of
wine. Great. There was too much food. She would be re-heating the same
meal for the next week—an unappetizing prospect.

She decided to go out for a walk and watch a heartwarming Thanksgiving special that was on later and go to bed early. The long weekend
stretched ahead, and she didn't want to think about that right now. She
needed to mentally commune with the American people.

There was a light snow outside, a whisper of winter ahead, and the
black streetlamps, hung with red ribbons and individual, fresh-looking
wreaths, looked a little like something out of Dickens. Given momentary
pause, she hoped her part in the world was not that of Ebenezer Scrooge,
although she knew some people at the Democratic Club thought of her
that way.

"Is that you, Helene?"

She turned and squinted through the snow. It was Arlene Wolff, who
worked for the city. In fact, Arlene had quite a position of importance in
the city as an assistant to the Mayor. Her position was earned through
extremely hard workhorse labor, with responsibilities nobody else wanted
devolving down to her. Helene had seen Arlene at the Democratic Club
a few times. To her knowledge, Arlene had managed, during an economic
downtown, to become a one-woman show at the Department of Civic
Affairs and Public Events. Practically everyone except Arlene had been
fired. A secretary, Arlene understood the department better than anyone
else, and she was left to run the whole department herself. With nothing
but grit and a willingness to put herself on the line, Arlene managed to
finagle merchants and property owners to contribute to work with their
communities to institute city-wide celebrations for every holiday known

to man, creating a festive communal atmosphere. Helene supposed she owed the red ribbons and fresh wreaths on the lampposts to Arlene's efforts.

"Yes, it's me," she answered courteously. She respected Arlene's civic-mindedness. "What are you doing this fine Thanksgiving evening?"

"Walking my dog."

"Oh."

"What are you doing?"

"Walking myself," said Helene.

As the two stopped to converse, it turned out that Arlene had no family or friends in the area either. Work had consumed her, and she had no time for a social life. She hadn't even cooked a turkey. In fact, she was trying to find a deli or something that was open all night to buy herself a turkey sandwich in honor of the holiday.

Helene stuttered," I cooked a turkey. There's way too much for me. I'll bet it's still warm. Would you care to have Thanksgiving Dinner with me?" She winked conspiratorially. "I even have a bottle of wine."

Arlene said she had to get her dog back, but in a moment of largesse very unlike her usual self, Helene said the dog could come up into her apartment while they were dining.

That quiet little evening—two women alone in a small apartment on Lenox Hill, dining over a single candle and confiding in one another their lives—was the beginning of a friendship that was to span the next several decades of their lives.

Helene's heart was singing. "I'm not alone! I have a friend! I have someone to feast with!"

Outside, the black lampposts glowed and lit up the falling snowflakes. Had anyone glanced up at Helene's third floor window from the lamp-lit street with the swirling snow, they would have seen sparkling warm light emanating from the windows and heard the laughter of newfound friendship, punctuated by the clink of wineglasses and the occasional bark of a dog.

To Helene, Arlene's awesome talents in the performance of her civic duties and her selfless devotion to the City of New York were equaled only by her talent for selfless and devoted friendship. Helene had never dreamed such a friendship was possible. The word "generosity" didn't begin to describe the benefits of being good friends with Arlene Wolff.

If Arlene baked bread, she brought half of it over to Helene's apartment to share. If she had tickets to an event (she got many free tickets through her position in the Mayor's office) Helene was always first on the list to be invited to go along. Helene attended banquets and museum openings and building dedications and all kinds of civic and cultural events in the great city of New York, always at the side of her friend, Arlene. Her life became exciting. She truly became part of the city, something she had always yearned for through her service at the Democratic Club. The Mayor started nodding to her in recognition, as did many other city luminaries. Life was good.

Looking over Helene's portfolio of articles one day, Arlene was delighted by the captions and little explanations Helene had tagged to each one, strictly for her own amusement. Arlene encouraged Helene to accompany her little stories when she submitted them to editors to see if they would publish her words. Helene agreed to try. She had more than enough work these days, as Arlene threw business her way from her many contacts in the city, and now Arlene threw even more business her way since she was beginning to submit written pieces.

Helene's finances thrived, and she redecorated her apartment, with Arlene's opinion guiding her all along the way. She thought of purchasing a small car, but it was too impractical in the city. Instead, she returned Arlene's generosity by paying for a weekend at an upstate spa at a lake resort. They had mud baths and facials, lolled around the sauna in thick towels, swam and ate and read to their hearts' content, sharing a beautiful suite of rooms. Helene even paid for Arlene's dog-sitter. It was one of the most memorable weekends in either of their hard-working lives—to be completely and utterly pampered by the full staff of a place devoted to luxurious care.

People at the Democratic Club commented that Helene looked and acted younger now that she had a close friend. She was in the habit of throwing her head back and laughing thunderously at even small jokes. She was happy, and some of Arlene's kindness and diplomacy from her high level job were rubbing off on her. She was a better president of the Club because of Arlene's influence.

Then the unthinkable happened. Arlene met a man—a man she really, really liked. Helene tried to take it with good grace.

They were feminists, both of them, who believed in Gloria Steinem's dictum: "A woman needs a man like a fish needs a bicycle." But all that didn't matter much when Tom Pettlinson walked into the Democratic Club one evening and, very politely, asked if he could be of service to the Club. He was a tweedy, professorial type but attractive nonetheless. Helene appraised him. He was nice-enough looking, although not handsome enough to be a threat to anyone. He was certainly polite. His responses to her questions showed an informed and intelligent mind and a gentle, caring character. Helene said crisply that if he was willing to show up for meetings—which could only be proven over time—they might be able to use him as a door-to-door canvasser.

Arlene, listening and looking on, began to act as if she were flustered. Helene stared at her. She had never seen Arlene flustered by anything. Then she understood. Arlene found Tom attractive. If nearly uninterrupted eye contact meant anything, the feeling was returned.

Arlene fell for Tom like a ton of bricks. Helene was patient with what she considered a mid-life crush and was indulgent with Arlene when she wanted his contact information from Helene and insisted that they take their evenings walks with Campbell (Arlene's dog) in front of Tom's apartment building. When they ran into him one evening, the spark of mutual interest between Arlene and Tom burst into a flame. Helene definitely felt like a third wheel. Falling in love at their age was nonsense. Of course, Arlene was younger than she was, but Arlene had been married, divorced, and had children in college, for goodness sake. Love was for the young. Middle-aged and older women were more properly devoted to love of causes, Helene thought.

It was insane to be jealous, Helene knew. Her friendship with Arlene had never had a tinge of dependency about it. It had just been fun, intellectually stimulating, and had been, Helene felt, a reward for her years of devotion to selfless causes. Arlene had practically given her the key to the city, which Helene thought she deserved.

Of course, now the free tickets to concerts, museum openings, cultural events, and fundraisers went mostly to Tom, who accompanied Arlene. They were a couple. Arlene was too kind and fair not to include Helene whenever she could, even sacrificing a date with Tom to take Helene to an event, but the old, easy fun times they used to have seemed to be behind them. Helene could sense Arlene was restless at these events, wishing she were with Tom instead of Helene.

Glowing with the thrill of being in love, Arlene looked young and well. She began to style her hair carefully, wear makeup, and choose fashionable clothing. Helene went about stubbornly make-upless, wearing dowdy clothes that looked as if she couldn't care less about her appearance (she couldn't). Yet she suddenly felt old and outdated and possibly irrelevant.

She wondered if Tom and Arlene would marry.

Of course, she and Arlene still saw one another frequently. They lived within a block of one another. Arlene would pop over with a freshly baked loaf of bread like she always had, or a half a steak, but she would talk of nothing but what she and Tom were going to do that evening or weekend and seemed absent-minded. On holidays, she went with Tom to visit his family, who lived in Connecticut. Arlene and Helene had made several holidays together, decorating and baking treats that they distributed at the Democratic Club or attended a stellar, glistening city holiday event. Now Helene was alone again.

Helene steeled herself with self-discipline and silently wished the couple well. She was gracious to both of them, occasionally having a candlelight dinner for them in her apartment, playing the role of a servant while they dined at a small table she set up with a white tablecloth in the living room for them. Her protests were loud when Arlene said things like, "I hope you don't mind. I asked Tom to attend that concert at the Lincoln Center with me. I know you like Bach, but I was only able to get one extra ticket . . . "

"Of course," Helene always said graciously. She made excuses like, "I'm busy myself. That new committee at the Club just isn't getting off the ground, and I need to meet with them."

Loneliness had moved back into Helene's life. Arlene knew it, pretended she didn't know it, and nodded as if that new committee at the Club just couldn't get along without Helene's intervention. Arlene wanted to be with Tom. She couldn't help herself.

Now that she had tasted the joys of friendship, Helene decided that the answer to her pain and loneliness was to cultivate more friends. She thought that was a healthy response to the challenge. She had learned that Ralph Waldo Emerson was right: to have a friend, you needed to be a friend. She worked hard to control her irascibility and sarcasm at the Club. She became kinder. It was a natural place to make friends with so much in common—and she often had guests over to her apartment for dinners, drinks, teas, or dessert.

It was the young people who responded to her most. Helene didn't know why, and she was absurdly happy when a note of envy came into Arlene's voice when she mentioned how drawn the young generation of Leftists were to Helene. They made Helene feel vital, alive, and valuable as they gathered around her to listen to her wisdom. She had lived through the Roaring Twenties, the Depression, World War II, the Korean War, and now Vietnam. She regaled them with details of what life was like during all those eras, speaking frankly and wittily, and the young people laughed and laughed, claiming that spending time with her should be worth some credits at nearby Columbia University.

What was more, Helene was courageous and outspoken and probably more left wing and a great deal more informed than many of them were. She absolutely despised the Vietnam War and was voluble about it. They listened to her with rapt attention, especially the young men who were eligible for the draft. They didn't want to go to war, and Helene's diatribes against the war made them feel that they shouldn't go, shouldn't take part in something so venal and awful. She had quite a following, and she was always ready to lead them in a demonstration, in canvassing the public, and to fearlessly speak out on the steps of public buildings, particularly at Columbia.

The girls admired her because she could tell them how life was for a girl growing up in the early decades of the century—how restrictive the clothing was, how restrictive were the manners and mores. Her biting wit and sense of irony made them laugh. It was funny to hear someone in her mature years use salty language and speak so honestly. The girls were her followers too, and they confided in her all their travails with their young men and careers. Many of them were university students, and through them Helene had easy access to the campus.

Her life was growing fuller. She treasured her friendship with Arlene, but it had been a stepping stone to more relationships, combating the deep-seated loneliness in her life. She felt she owed Arlene a lot, but she had become truly generous about Arlene's relationship with Tom.

When Tom and Arlene split up, Helene, who would have welcomed such news before, was only concerned with her friend's state of heart and mind. She felt no self-satisfaction or hope for a renewal of the intensity of their friendship in the pre-Tom days. She was worried about Arlene's depression.

Arlene had given her a great deal, and Helene did not think it was beyond what she owed her to include her in her soirées for young people at her apartment or to invite her to campus events. Now it was Arlene who looked enviously and wistfully at Helene's life and wished she had not limited herself so to one person, one man. Now Helene was her lifeline.

Time heals all wounds. Arlene eventually recovered from her disappointment over Tom and balanced her life well between various new friendships and civic work. Helene's and Arlene's friendship became an important part of their lives, not the whole for either of them. It worked better that way. Helene always had invitations for the holidays now or was entertaining in her apartment. She would ask Arlene along if it seemed appropriate, and other times she didn't. They were mature, independent women, and life had toughened both of them up. They could face some loneliness at times, for their lives were full of rewards and relationships.

Although Arlene still threw work her way, Helene found walking around the city in search of good material to write about was wearing on her knees, which were beginning to sound a few notes of the sour music of arthritis. She spent more and more time at her desk, writing. She wrote her autobiography and shopped it around to the New York publishers, but no one was interested. She was not famous, not beautiful, not scandalous, not excessively good nor excessively evil, not powerful. No one would want to read about her, even if she had spent almost a lifetime observing the country and changing along with it.

"I am living history," she complained to Arlene. "And no one wants to know about it."

Now her income was reduced as she wrote and sold fewer and fewer pieces and as her writing had been taken up with her unsold autobiography. She tried her hand at plays—she would love to see her words enacted by real people on a real stage—but no one was buying any of that either.

Arlene managed to get her a commission to write about the young people she held her soirées for—their ideals and idealism, what motivated them, what their backgrounds were, what their impressions and goals for America truly were. She could include photos, taken right in her own apartment or out on the street, with the students leaning casually against the lampposts. It was a goldmine for Helene.

The retrospective book took her two years to write, and a good paycheck from the cultural center sponsoring the project came in every two weeks. The fact that she was studying them and writing a book about them attracted more and more young people to her apartment, trying to get their stories told. Helene realized that, no matter how rebellious any person might be, he or she wanted to be heard, to be known, to be listened to—even to be loved. It was a bit of wisdom about human nature she tucked away in her mind. It was true of her too. No matter how much she railed against society, society was what she needed. She needed and wanted others in her life. Satisfying relationships were the fabric of life.

As she cultivated the art of listening, she made more and more friends and had more influence at the Democratic Club.

"You don't say anything, and yet everyone wants your opinion!" Arlene semi-complained.

"Everyone loves a listener," Helene told her. "You taught me that!"

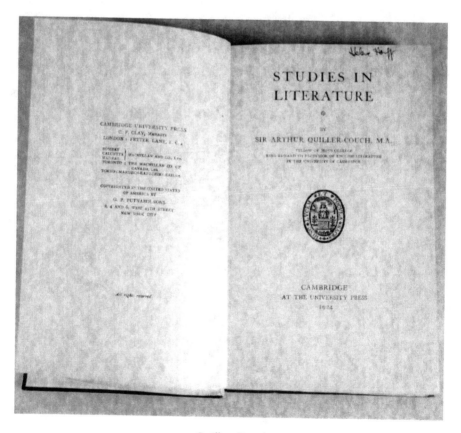

Quiller-Couch

OUR NATION'S
CAPITAL

by Helene Hanff

NELSON DOUBLEDAY, INC. · GARDEN CITY, N.Y.

A Hanff History Book

CHAPTER 11

She was supposed to get royalties for the retrospective book about the radicals and rebels of the 1960s (called *Movers and Shakers* to demonstrate the young people's impatience with things as they were and their desire for rapid change). She had thought the royalties would help keep her for the rest of her life. She was full of energy, but she was getting older. She had to think of the future. Then Arlene had to inform her, sadly, that the cultural center that had commissioned the book had decided not to publish it. They were low on funds, and the country was in no mood to read the histories of young demonstrators and radicals. There was no interest in bringing the book out, as there was no audience for it. The manuscript would simply be archived.

Helene asked if she could try to get *Movers and Shakers* published herself, by one of the New York publishing houses. She'd already gone that route with her own autobiography and was not enthused about attempting it again. The queries, the Xeroxing, the packaging everything up (and that cost something too) and sending it out, the endless waiting only to be met with rejection slip after rejection slip did not appeal to her. Yet she was desperate for income. She tried a few queries here and there, and they all said the same thing: now the country wanted to move on, out of the Sixties.

She had no income and plenty of bills. She was now over sixty, and it was going to be very hard to find a job. She went over to Arlene's to plead for more city work, but Arlene told her that budgets were tight and she couldn't offer her any.

"You're all right, though, aren't you? I mean, you've been saving all this time, haven't you?"

"Oh, sure," Helene lied. She had not. She had spent a lot of her money on entertaining and donating to the causes she believed in. She wondered what she was going to do.

Then Arlene told her that she was moving to Florida. Arlene's elderly mother was failing in health and needed someone to take care of her. Arlene was going to move in with her as a full-time caregiver. This was another blow, although Helene was relieved that Arlene was not going to be there to watch what she perceived was going to be a long, economical downfall for Helene.

Helene wandered the streets, wondering what to do. She had way too much experience to accept just any job. At the same time, she was too old for many human resources people. In her life, she had experienced a lot of "isms". There wasn't even a term for "ageism" then but everyone knew what it was. The raven-haired person got the job before the grey-haired one.

Her pride kept her from telling her many acquaintances and contacts that she actually needed a job. She'd had something of an unspoken reputation as being someone's rich divorced wife or widow—independently wealthy—who did civic work out of a liberal sense of duty. No one but Arlene had known how hard she had to work all these years.

She took to walking more and more often, mostly to avoid the collection agency phone calls that were beginning to bombard her at her apartment. She had stopped paying her bills. She was not sure how long it would be before she was evicted. She was glad Arlene was not there to see it.

When someone at the Democratic Club would offer to go out and get doughnuts, she tried not to show her teeth in a feral, hungry grin, nodding. Sometimes doughnuts were all she had for dinner these days.

She gambled a few of her last dollars on an ad in the newspaper for a moving sale and some construction paper to make signs to put up in Laundromats and public places. It worked out well. Many people came to her apartment, and she sold almost everything she had, except for a couple of changes of clothes. Her cameras fetched a pretty sum.

When that money ran out, she took to hanging around the subway stations at night to keep warm. She used the restrooms in the museums (she never donated the suggested amount and bore the glares of the young women behind the greeting counters bravely). She washed up in public restrooms, ignoring the repelled stares of other patrons as she washed out the armpits of a sweater and dried it under the hot-air hand dryer. It was so warm and clean in places like the museums, and she could sit on a bench all day, gazing at a painting. She thought of hiding somewhere in the museums at night so as to be able to spend the nights out of the weather, but she was too frightened. She might get in trouble with the police.

She actually did get in trouble with the police while walking over the Columbia University campus one day. Campuses were good places if you were homeless, if you could ignore the bold stares and uncensored comments of young people when they happened upon a bag lady. A person could stay in the library for long periods of time, and the buildings looked more susceptible to night hiding than the museum buildings did. She did notice that she was asked to leave places more often than before, as her clothes got dirtier and more raggedy-looking. Now people knew she was homeless, not just someone who was hanging around. She told them she was researching a book on student activism, called *Movers and Shakers*. That was the name of the book she had been writing for the cultural center.

No one believed her. They didn't say anything, but she could see how they rolled their eyes skeptically and then told her, with an air of superiority, that she had to leave.

"I all but owned this City once," she silently screamed at them. "You should have seen the glittering events I went to—I sat right next to the Mayor!"

She was just walking along on campus when she saw someone she knew in the crowd of an anti-Vietnam War demonstration taking place on one of the main building's front steps. She started waving frantically. She thought it was a student she had invited over to her apartment quite a few times, and she was wondering if he might be good for a few dollars if she asked—and then a policeman grabbed her waving arm and used it to strong-arm her into a waiting car. They were arresting other people too. In the squad car, she understood that they thought she was trying to throw a Molotov cocktail. She was disappointed when the charges were dismissed and she was asked to leave the station. She had been hoping to stay overnight in a warm cell, sleep on a cot, and be fed.

She was so lonely, she went into a phone booth and began thumbing through the thick phone book. Maybe she would spot a name she knew, a name she remembered. She had a little change. She could make a phone call: ask for help.

She hadn't dared show her face at the Democratic Club, poor as she now was. She felt ashamed to be seen in her tattered coat and scuffed up boots, one of which had developed a big blooming hole in the side that was terribly visible. For all their dedication to "humanity," she could not imagine them caring for a woman who had fallen down from a high position to a low one because she had run out of gas in her career and was growing old alone. And the City—once completely open to her—was absolutely merciless when a person was down. She'd found that out.

To comfort herself—it was cold in the phone booth—she flipped to the Ms and looked for "Arlene Wolff." Of course, there were pages and pages of Wolffs, but she was surprised to find a distinct "Arlene M. Wolff" among the many names. Wasn't Arlene's middle name Marie?

This must be an old phone book, she reasoned, but the address wasn't the same. This address was near their old neighborhood but not in it. To her knowledge, Arlene had never lived there. Maybe she lived there now?

The old force of their friendship—how she could tell Arlene almost anything and be accepted and understood—rose up in her heart. She gambled her last change on the phone call, shaking her head at herself and feeling her heart beat so hard she could feel it in her throat.

She was shocked when Arlene's voice answered the phone.

"Arlene?"

"Helene! Is that you?"

"Is that you, Arlene? What are you doing in New York?"

"My mother died. I came back to the city I love. Mom left me quite an inheritance, and I can afford to live where I want. Where are you? I've been trying and trying to find you!"

Arlene had walked around their old neighborhood, asking anyone and everyone if they knew where Helene had gone. All anyone could tell her was that Helene had sold everything she owned and moved away. Arlene had asked around the Democratic Club, and people said they had not seen Helene for ages. Arlene had even gone to Columbia University and walked around, looking for familiar faces of students who had known Helene and been to her apartment. No luck. Everyone they had known had graduated by then.

Helene slumped against the side of the phone booth, wondering what more to say. She didn't have a lot of pride left, but it was hard to ask for help. She believed in and had worked for a society where everyone helped one another; especially where the rich helped the poor. Arlene was rich. She was destitute. Why wouldn't her old friend help her? She clung to the phone as if to a lifeline, but she couldn't bring herself to ask Arlene for help.

Wisely, Arlene did not ask about her circumstances. Somehow, she sensed them. Arlene ascertained Helene's location and told her to wait for her there.

"Better yet, isn't there a restaurant nearby? Honor's Place? I know where that is. Okay, go in there and order some food. My treat. I'll join you in about fifteen minutes."

Helene saw the looks they gave her at Honor's Place. They did not want to let her in to sit down, but she mentioned Arlene's name. Fortunately, the restaurant owner remembered Arlene from her community work long ago, and he tentatively agreed to seat Helene, off in the corner where she wouldn't be very noticeable, for a time. He even charitably decided to give her whatever she ordered.

Arlene gasped but covered it up when she saw Helene. How old Helene had become! Old and raggedy-looking. She came to the table, sumptuously dressed, and chatted away as if nothing had changed between them.

Finally, Helene said, simply, "I couldn't find work."

"The city can be brutal," Arlene nodded. "We'll get you on your feet, though."

Arlene called a taxi for them both. Helene sat shivering in the cab, her teeth almost chattering. She was going to have a warm place to sleep tonight. She was going to have food and coffee, and she was going to be helped, as she had tried so hard to help others in her own idealistic way.

The city was an expensive place to live. Through her multiple contacts, Arlene was able to help Helene find a job in a small town several hours out of the city. An elderly official had retired there, and he was quite influential in the town. It was in a rural area, and rents were low. Arlene drove Helene out into the country and introduced her to the librarian, who was retiring and who also ran the local newspaper. Arlene explained Helene's strong civic and literary background, and it was agreed: Helene would become the new librarian-cum-newspaper-editor-in-chief. The salary offered by the town was not enough money to live on, but Arlene lied and told Helene that an apartment's rent was included in the deal, courtesy of the municipality. Then she made a secret deal with the influential official that she herself would pay Helene's rent, unbeknownst to Helene.

To their delight, they found a farmhouse on an acre of land that had been converted into apartments. The old white house, built to withstand the winds, had been standing for one hundred years. Arlene and Helene gazed at it a long time. Helene's apartment was one of four; it was a first floor apartment with a simple, small, cottagey aspect to it, sheltered under the oaken wings of the big house.

"This house has withstood many storms and winds," the proprietor assured Helene.

"So have I," she said. "We'll get along."

The rest of the farmhouse was rented out to college students, as there was a small, elite university in a nearby town. Helene knew she would fit right in there.

"Students are much more conservative these days," Arlene warned her. "But I'm sure they'll like you. They always have. And it's a perfect place to write and take photos."

Helene had never thought she would like rural life, but she did. Maybe because now she was slowing down, the pace of life suited her better than life in the city. She felt part of nature here, and in nature, things grew old, withered, and eventually fell off the vine. Decaying flowers comforted her. Growing old and physically declining was a part of life.

She took long walks, looking at cows and horses in the fields, and returned to her converted farmhouse apartment to write and plan what photos she would take that afternoon, when the sun was strong. That was on her day off. During the week, she was busy at the library and running the newspaper.

She had never been happier. She made friends with Arlene's contact who had gotten her the job and became active in local politics. The (sometimes irascible) old liberal with the heart of kindness became something of a fixture and an institution in the town.

Her only concern was how to pay back Arlene. Not in money, of course, but for all she had done for her and taught her over the years. There was only one thing she could think of: Tom. Arlene still sometimes mentioned him when she came out of the city to visit. Helene's active and activist life amused her, in addition to how well Helene had taken to small country town living. She visited most Sundays, and from her conversation, Helene could tell Arlene was still carrying the torch for Tom.

Helene did everything she could to follow every possible lead on where Tom might be these days. In those pre-Internet days, it was not easy. Yet Helene had a "nose for a story" as people in the town said of her newspaper work. She began to devote a lot of her free time to making phone calls and writing letters. Finally, she got an address which she hoped belonged to him. She wrote him a note, gave him a free subscription to the newspaper, and followed it up with several lengthy letters about Arlene and all Arlene had done for her. She did not hold back about her period of homelessness and how generous Arlene had been. She described Arlene's sacrificial service to her mother in her dying years as well as depicting, more than Tom probably ever knew, how much Arlene had served the City of New York.

He did not reply. Helene didn't know if she was sending the materials out into a black void or not. Maybe the Tom Pettlinson she was writing to was not the same one Arlene had known and loved.

Helene didn't tell anyone, but she was starting to experience more exhaustion than even her advancing years called for. There was the dizziness too, and the headaches, and the feelings that something was draining, draining, draining, deep within her. She did not tell Arlene. She did not want Arlene to worry about her. Kind, generous Arlene, whose forehead was beginning to crease with age and loneliness—Helene never told her anything upsetting. She certainly did not tell her about her search for Tom.

Then it happened. Helene collapsed on one of her country walks. It was her heart. Some children playing in a nearby field spotted the heaped up bundle of clothing on the road and called their mother, who called the police. The town had no hospital; Helene was taken by squad car to the nearest city. She thought amusedly, before she slipped into unconsciousness, that the police owed her this trip anyway for having once arrested her for no reason.

As the lights in the hospital grew dimmer and dimmer in her failing sight, and she felt the draining sensation beginning to take her down a whirling vortex into the unknown, she wished with all her soul that Arlene would find the happiness she deserved. Her attempts to locate Tom to affect a reunion had been fruitless, but she had tried. All she could do now was, with her last breath, to wish happiness for her kind and generous friend, who was, even then, rushing to the hospital to pay Helene's bill.

Heartbreak Thursday

CHAPTER 12

SP: You've told me many times how much you enjoy Broadway shows.

HH: I do, I do.

SP: What is about them that you like?

HH: I know where you're heading with this, Mr. Skeptic.

SP: Oh, that's good to know. Do you have a crystal ball hidden in with your Marlboros?

HH: (Laughing). That would be great, wouldn't it?

SP: So what's with Broadway?

HH: It's light and airy and silly and endearing and the stage is full of cute, talented people, singing their way through life.

SP: You could say the same thing about the Mormon Tabernacle Choir.

HH: But I didn't, wise-guy. I like musicals because they hearken back to simpler times, I guess. How can you not love Ethel Merman?

SP: Pretty easily. I had an aunt that shouted almost as loudly and I didn't tap my foot to her ranting.

HH: You're just being argumentative. You obviously don't like musicals and I do and there's nothing you can say that will change my mind.

SP: Actually, I was hoping you would change my mind.

HH: Sure. Like Castro changing Nixon's mind. Did Nixon have a mind?

SP: I voted for him.

HH: Well I voted for Castro.

It was 4.30 pm on a cloudy October afternoon. Helene finished her second cup of tea and started gathering her notes. Her small coffee table was almost buried under them, which was only natural, considering that the elections were only a month away. She had spent most of the afternoon going over her notes and planning the evening meeting at her Democratic local club which was only a few blocks away from her apartment. Helene liked walking to the club; it gave her the opportunity of organizing her ideas and of interacting with some of the neighbors, especially a couple of middle-aged women who were still reluctant to attend meetings and events. It was difficult for them to understand why Helene was so involved in politics and social causes. Even if the ladies from Lenox Hill led an active social life they almost never attended political meetings so some of them thought Helene was friendly and outgoing but yet "strange"Helene was looking forward to this meeting because Mollie, a housewife and mother of two college students had accepted to go with her. Helene had talked to her trying to explain her point of view: that they were already in the sixties and the new generation expected their elders to be more involved and informed.

She smiled to herself remembering her little "speech" and as she turned around the corner of her street block she saw Mollie with two stiff looking older ladies. Mollie smiled at her and introduced the ladies as her aunts Laura and Pam. "This is becoming interesting" though Helene as she led the group towards the club. While walking to the club, Helene tried to engage in conversation with her peculiar group but all she could obtain was Mollie's nervous giggling and a blank stare from the two old ladies. She felt a little nervous but was hoping that the club's fast pace would cheer them up. Lenox Hill local Democratic Club was a brick one storied building with a wide driveway. In the back yard there were two pines, a weeping willow tree, long benches and a medium sized barbecue. A couple of fund-raising barbecues had already taken place there, with acceptable outcome; now Helene was planning a major one just before election day and hoping it would be successful. The club was very busy: the telephones were constantly ringing, a group of teens was painting some campaign signs and the "campaign committee" was having a heated discussion and flipping papers over. Helene approached them and introduced the new comers. After a few smiles and hand shaking the commotion started again: a young girl was shouting over the phone and ended hanging it up furiously. Helene was shocked and even more so seeing Mollie go towards the girl and start calming her down. After a few minutes Mollie picked up the phone, made a call and announced;" Helene, the survey will be ready tomorrow as promised" Helene was pleased but as she turned again to the "committee" she bumped into the two aunts. They were standing in the middle of the room wide-eyed.

She led them towards a small desk and asked them to sit down and to make a list of all the people they knew liked the open air and barbecues. Helene and her fellow partisans believed that socializing helped politics so they thoroughly planned the different events. They also knew that the work would not be over after election day, much on the contrary, they would continue seeing to the different issues whether their candidate was elected to the State Senate or not.

They were also ready to elect new authorities because their current president was too busy seeing to his business to dedicate so much time to the club. Although he had promised to keep in contact as much as possible, they were sad to see him resign: he was an active man in his sixties who had always vehemently supported the Party.

That evening he asked for everybody's attention and announced he was sad to resign. He suggested they should take a moment to elect his successor so they could continue with the work.

They did not take long organizing the election and after a few minutes the former president said: "My friends, I am proud to present the new president...Ms Helene!" Almost everybody started clapping, almost everybody but one little lady, aunt Betty, who stood up and shouted: "A woman! President of a political club!!!!???" They all looked at her waiting for the worst but she simply tried to compose herself and added emotionally: "I have finally found my local club!"

It was a big evening for everybody especially for the women who saw that for the first time after many years of dedicated effort a woman had been elected president of the Democratic local club. Helene felt honored and a bit overwhelmed but she accepted the nomination because, in the end, politics and social causes were her life.

Helene was very much involved in partisan politics but that was not her only interest. She was also concerned with social issues, especially those regarding women, youth and minorities. She also thought of herself as a writer but had not been lucky so far. The publishers she had visited had told her that her books were too deep for the average public and would not sell. Even so, she had not given up and continued doing research and jotting down notes in the hopes of seeing her works published one day.

Helene agreed that it was important for people to enjoy themselves and to find different ways of distraction but she also believed education and knowledge provided joy and freedom of thought. She used to tell the young people she met at meetings and social events: "the more you learn, the better equipped you are to build your destiny."

Although the educational problems found during the fifties in secondary schools were being solved by having returned to teaching the primary skills, she wondered to what extent minorities actually benefited from the educational system. "Well...I will start seeing to that tomorrow" she thought as she turned her night lamp off. Helene felt very happy tonight, it had been a good day: new members for the club and the pride of having been elected president!

The next day, while preparing coffee, she heard a soft knock at her door. She looked through the peep-hole but did not see anybody. As she was turning away, she noticed a small slip of paper half way under the door. She picked it up, unfolded it and read: "We are watching you, lady!". At first she was nervous but then she thought that as elections were so close it could be a silly joke and tossed it into her handbag without giving it a second thought.

As she was going to meet the principal of the local high school, after taking a shower she decided to wear a tailored suit and high heels. She knew her feet would hurt most of the morning but she wanted to look classy.

Twenty minutes later Helene got in her small red car and after driving a few blocks she noticed that a white sedan had been behind her all the time. She told herself not to be paranoid, brushed the thought away and finally parked at the site reserved for visitors.

The meeting with the principal was interesting; she learned there were not many students per class and that there was still a lot of work that needed to be done to improve the learning process. Helene was offered a tour around school and was not surprised at not seeing many minorities. She made a comment to the principal who simply shrugged and said they could go to their own schools. Helene was expecting this type of comment and smiled to herself because for all she knew the city of New York was not planning to build more schools. She thought about discussing the issue at the club's meeting that night and that they could probably help her come up with a good plan of action.

She was still thinking about it when, on approaching her car she noticed she had a flat tire. She sighed looking at her high heels and skirt but quickly took her shoes off and started changing it. While working on the tire she heard a click close to her left ear but when she looked up she only saw a man going past her and smoking a cigar. "That sounded like a camera" she thought as she stood up looking around her. Except for that man nobody else was walking by so she decided she should cut back on coffee drinking because it was starting to get on her nerves. When she got in her car, Helene remembered the note and the white Sedan but convinced herself they were simple coincidences.

Once in her apartment Helene took a long shower and feeling hungry decided to eat a big piece of pumpkin pie and to drink a glass of milk. She started reading some notes on education while she ate but was soon very sleepy so she went to bed for a short nap. The telephone woke her up but when she answered it, whoever it was, quickly hung up.

Once on the street and on her way to the club she saw a young woman in a ponytail jogging in her same direction. Helene thought she should probably start doing the same or forget all about pies. To her surprise, the young woman continued jogging and turned in the direction of the local club. When she arrived she saw her at the front desk talking to the receptionist who said: "Helene, I would like you to meet Ms Rhoda Martin, assistant to the Major of New York".

They started talking and Helene was captivated by her personality; she thought that a woman who dared to go jogging all by herself in those times was definitely very special. It was easy for Rhoda to interact with the rest of the team: she was friendly, easy-going and very sure of herself. She told Helene they were actually neighbors and that she had seen her at the baker's many times because she lived on her same block. Helene and Rhoda were animatedly talking when Mollie approached them with the evening paper in her hand. There it was: a picture of Helene fighting a tire and a caption that read: "female mechanic-activist". Everybody started talking at the same time, some of them even suggested contacting the editor and asking for an explanation and apsociety

ology but Rhoda said that in the end, instead of being upset they should take it as a good piece of free propaganda. Helene liked the idea and thought it would still be interesting to talk to the editor and find out if they could have his support in future activities.

During the evening meeting, Helene also mentioned her interview with the school principal and especially her comments on minorities. One of the teenagers who had been working on the signs said that his neighbors were from South America and owned a small coffee shop close to his house. It was decided to get in touch with them and explore the possibility of having a meeting regarding school opportunities.

It was a good and productive evening: they even had time to discuss the final big barbecue and were glad to learn that Mollie's aunts had produced quite a long list of relatives and friends who they were already contacting.

After the meeting Helene and Rhoda walked back home together. Despite the age difference they clearly enjoyed each other's company . They were both energetic and talkative and what Helene liked the most about her was the passion and her apparent unconditional desire to help people.

As they lived on the same block Helene invited Rhoda over so they could have coffee together and some dessert. When Helene opened the front door she saw another piece of paper; this time it read: "You made it home safe, for now." They looked at each other unable to react. A few seconds later Rhoda almost whispered that she thought Helene should call the police. Helene turned pale and sat down at the kitchen table without a word. Her mind was racing remembering the previous note and the Sedan behind her. She could see Rhoda's lips moving but could not hear her offering a glass of water.

She finally drank it slowly and told her the whole story showing her the first slip of paper. Rhoda wanted to stay with her overnight but Helene reassured her she was fine and that it was not necessary. Even so, she had to promise to lock herself up and to go to the police station first thing the next morning.

That night she could hardly sleep because she kept on thinking about the different meetings she had held, trying to imagine who could wish to hurt her. She finally had to admit that there were many possibilities especially in those times and for a couple of minutes she actually thought she had not been too smart when she had "gladly" decided to face "whatever it took" in the pursuit of her ideals. Tonight, lying in bed and paying attention to the slightest noise, she certainly wished her ideals would get her out of this situation.

She had not slept long when early the next morning she was woken up by someone pounding at her door. Looking through the peep-hole she saw an agitated Rhoda and the property manager who looked as if he really did not want to be there. When she opened the door Rhoda stormed in followed by the unhappy-looking manager who was carrying a form. He informed that because of Rhoda's "hysterical concern" he had to inspect the premises as such were the "procedures." Helene was too tired to argue so she let him do it secretly wishing they would leave and let her go back to bed.

Once the manager had finished his inspection he left the apartment mumbling to himself and as Helene stood up to go back to her bedroom she was stopped by an angry Rhoda who said: "Where do you think you are going? Get dressed! We are going to the police station!" Once on their way, Rhoda talked non-stop while Helene simply dozed off.

The traffic was unusually heavy that morning; they were wondering about the reason when they were forced to come to a stop.

At first they did not understand what was going on but then they heard the chanting, yelling and blowing of horns. It was a medium-sized demonstration; people were walking, chanting and clapping their hands. They tried hard to listen but it was impossible because the drivers were getting impatient and kept on blowing their horns.

Helene jumped out of the car and ran the two blocks that separated them from the demonstrators. Then she saw the big signs: "Equal education opportunities now!" Most of the demonstrators were African-American but Helene could also see a few Latinos. She grabbed one of the pamphlets they were handing out and started walking back towards the car. It was then when she heard the screech and the shouting; a furious driver had gone past them almost running a few over. Some drivers imitated him so the place became a complete mess; people were fighting, crying, shouting and running in all directions.

Things got worse when the police arrived; their presence seemed to upset not only the demonstrators but some on lookers as well so there was more fighting and running. Helene was trying to go back to the car when she saw a little boy crying for his mother. She tried to shield him with her body to prevent him from getting hurt and it was then when she felt strong fingers grabbing her right shoulder. It was a policeman who ordered her to walk towards a waiting police van. The little boy was taken away from her and when she demanded an explanation she was told to be silent and to wait until they arrived at the police station.

The van was crowded with sweaty and angry people. Some of them had bruises and torn shirts. Helene was wondering what could have happened to Rhoda; she was hoping she was safe and knew she would feel guilty if something bad had happened to her. To make matters worse, the slow ride to the police station was getting on her nerves.

At the police station the group was kept in a cell without further explanations. Half an hour later an officer ordered her to follow him and

Helene was thankful to see Rhoda standing at a desk with a grave looking young man.

The officer told her she was free to go and gave her a nasty look; Helene was ready to make a comment but Rhoda pulled her away and literally pushed her towards the exit. Once on the street the young man introduced himself as Martin and told her he was an attorney who worked for the city of New York.

According to Rhoda the policeman who had detained her thought she was going to hurt the little boy. Helene felt devastated and irritated so she decided to walk back into the police station to demand further explanations and to straighten matters up. Rhoda stopped her and told her she had been released so fast thanks to Martin and that she would be better off if she forgot the incident for the time being. Helene agreed reluctantly, not knowing that the "incident" as they called it, would fall back on her in the future.

Feeling they needed to calm down the group decided to have lunch together at an Italian little restaurant nearby. Fortunately the place was not too noisy so they could enjoy their conversation while they ate. Martin seemed to be interested in Helene's activities, especially those concerning the Democratic Party, so she invited her to join them at one of their meetings. He said he would be happy to go and that he was hoping to become an active member instead of simply sitting through the whole meeting. Helene liked his attitude and was happy at the idea of having the possibility of building a strong team. This is what society needs, she thought, dedicated and passionate people.

They were still talking animatedly and having a nice dessert when Helene exclaimed, "Wait a minute! I never told the police about the notes I have been getting!" Both she and Rhoda started laughing while Martin looked puzzled. Helene told him the story and he said he would like to take a look at the notes before getting in touch with some of his "contacts." Helene was glad: things seemed to be improving after all. After lunch they all went to work; Rhoda and Martin to their offices and Helene to the small public library where she worked part-time three afternoons a week. She had decided to take it up because it would help her pay her rent and some expenses as she had not been commissioned to do much research lately. College boards wanted objective research and writing and in the opinion of some of them Helene was becoming too much of an activist to be objective. She liked her job at the library which gave her the opportunity to interact with people and to study when she was not busy. She was hoping she would not be too busy this afternoon because she had quite a few things to plan: a meeting with the evening paper editor, a possible one concerning educational opportunities and the closing barbecue at her local club.

Helene was organizing a shelf when a group of young students came into the library. She thought she had seen a couple of them before but at first could not remember where. Then she did They had been together in the police van that morning! They did not notice her because they were too busy going up and down the aisles apparently looking for a particular book. When she offered to help them they told her they had to write an essay on the Bill of Rights. They seemed confused so Helene spent some time trying to help them. They had been talking for a while when one of them recognized her as well. They young boy looked as if he had met his soul mate and asked her if he could continue coming because he felt he could learn a lot from her comments. It was then when Helene's pride made her make a big mistake and accept.

When she left the library that evening she felt satisfied even if she had not had the chance to do any planning; she had spent an interesting afternoon talking to young people which she loved doing. The only problem was that she had failed to take into account that in those years and under the current social turmoil age difference mattered and could cause many problems.

She was home that night relaxing and watching the news when the telephone rang. She thought it could be from the club and was wondering if anything had gone wrong when she heard an unfamiliar voice on the other side. The lady told her she was Martina, and that her four children had been constantly rejected from Lenox High. Helene could not believe the coincidence; it was the school she had visited the previous day! Martina added as well that she knew at least four other ladies who had gone through the same situation. Helene told her she would be more than happy to meet her in person so they agreed to have breakfast together the next day, at a little "cafe" close to the "Evening Review." She was hoping to also be able to see the newspaper's editor before lunch, so that little cafe seemed to be the most convenient place to meet.

The next morning, when Helene arrived, Martina was already waiting for her; she was a middle-aged, dark-haired woman with a broad smile. Martina was from Venezuela and had lived in the USA for over twenty years. All her four children were American and had not had any problems during their elementary school years because they had attended a little school at their old neighborhood in a "Latino" community. Things had changed for her family when they decided to move to Lenox Hill. It had been hard to adapt to the new neighborhood; her children had almost no friends and were forced to travel a long distance to attend high school at the old neighborhood.

Martina told her that she had had several interviews with the school principal who had given her little excuses. She had even placed the children on a waiting list but had never called them back. Helene understood that the situation was unfair and frustrating but still wanted to know if Martina had been able to take any further steps to solve it.

She answered her that during their last interview she was so upset that she had accused the principal of discrimination but that she had looked at her mockingly and threatened to call the police if she dared to come back again.

That day Martina had left the high school in tears and had ran into an older lady who had tried her best to comfort her. It was then when she had learned that hers was not the only case. Martina had got in touch with the other families but so far none of them had been able to find a solution to their problem.

One of her friends from church has suggested she could go to the Democratic local club and find out if they were willing to help. She had been there the previous night and said that a young a nice secretary had given her Helene's telephone number.

Helene was very touched by this story; she also felt angry at the school principal and could not wait to start working on this case and to try to help to make things change for the better. In her opinion the timing was perfect because there were many groups fighting for their rights. All they needed was a good plan of action and followers. She asked Martina to keep in contact with the other families and reassured her that they would finally get the necessary help.

While she walked from the cafe to the newspaper's Helene was building a plan to help Martina and people in her situation; she would start by talking to the young boy from the club to see if they could get his group and Martina's together and hold a big meeting. Helene was excited and in good spirits when she arrived at the "Evening Review."

The place was busy; people were typing, talking on the phone and the editor was, of course, yelling behind his closed door. His secretary was a high school boy who tried to convince her to come some other time but Helene ignored him and led herself into his office. She told him right away that she was not happy with the picture of herself they had published to which he replied she should because it favored her, making her look a lot younger. It was definitely not a good start but Helene did not give up.

The editor's comments made Helene feel a little self-conscious. He was right, she was not a young woman anymore, she was in her mid-fifties and for a few seconds she wondered where all those years had gone. Yet, she was happy with her life; she considered herself very active and was in the end, steering her life the way she wanted to, or, at least, she thought so.

The editor was not paying attention to her anymore. In fact, he had picked up the phone and was scribbling something on a piece of paper. Helene sat down and waited. When he looked at her she simply smiled and told him she found the picture and caption embarrassing. He laughed saying that they had sold a lot of newspapers so she tried to take advantage of the comment and asked him if that meant they would support her cause.

The editor leaned back on his chair and told her that instead of worrying so much she should let events flow and pick the right opportunity. He added that when she thought about it she would understand that theirs or anybody's support depended only on herself. As she looked puzzled he said: "become an interesting character and we will unconditionally be there."

Helene left the building feeling happy and reassured: as he had said, it depended on her so she knew he would soon be on her side. Helene rushed back home; she had to get busy: the closing barbecue at the club would take place Friday night and there were still many details to see to. After a quick lunch she decided to call the presidents of the charity organizations that had already been invited and to give them a little reminder.

They would also have some entertainment and had contacted a jazz band so she decided to call Steve, the lead voice, to ask him if they were ready for the big day. Steve told her that they had been rehearsing a lot and that Friday she would be proud of them. Helene truly hoped so, especially because it had taken them a long time to come to an agreement on the kind of entertainment they would have. The teens had complained for hours because jazz was not their favorite style, they wanted something more "avant-garde" so they had had to explain to them that as most of the guests were middle-aged or older, the music should be as mellow as possible.

She also talked to the group of ladies in charge of making the center pieces for the tables and finally, as she had not heard from Rhoda since their "episode" at the demonstration, she also gave her a call. Rhoda told her she was busy preparing a festival the City would hold to honor its seniors but that she would do her best to join her at the club. That evening the club looked like a beehive: they were all busy seeing to the smallest detail. As they only had a day left before the big event, some had volunteered to spend it at the club. Helene was sad she was not going to be able to because she had to be at the library but was planning to leave as early as possible.

It was hard for Helene to concentrate on her work the next day. She did not really want to be at the library and the customers were getting on her nerves. She could not help but wonder how things were going at the club and kept on looking at her wristwatch.

The only highlight of the afternoon was the students' visit. Helene was glad to be able to concentrate on answering their various questions. They listened to her attentively and event took some notes. A couple of them asked her if they could still visit when they were done with the essay to which she responded that she would be more than glad to see them again.

They were about to leave when an elegant lady walked in. She was the mother of one of them who said she had been worrying all afternoon not knowing where he was. It did not matter to her that he was already a college boy; he lived with her and to her he was still her "little boy." The young man sighed and walked behind her. While they were leaving she eyed Helene from head to toe and coldly said: "Have a good night, Madam". Helene felt sorry for the student but quickly forgot about the incident because she could not wait to hear from the club.

She went by it right after work and was pleased to see that everything was almost ready and that it looked spotless clean. Mollie's two old aunts were thrilled because most of their friends had promised to attend. Even the members of the band had dropped by to get familiar with the place and to decide where to build a little stage. Everybody was exhausted so they decided to leave early and to get some rest because the next day was going to be extremely busy.

In the years to come Helene would always remember that day as one of the most important in her life.

The place was crowded, people were laughing, making new friends, talking politics, eating and having a wonderful time. The band was excellent; they played until late at night while couples danced and sang along. Even the teens who had complained so much had a wonderful time and declared later that jazz was not all that bad after all.

When the party was coming to an end Helene made a little speech saying that she was convinced their candidate would win. They all clapped and continued to enjoy the night.

Helene and Rhoda decided to take the weekend off and spent some time together going to the movies, to restaurants and shopping. The days seemed to rush by. Helene kept herself busy both at work and especially in politics, trying to raise as many votes as possible.

The college students continued visiting her at the library as promised and they all spent enlightening hours discussing different topics.

During those last days, the club members doubled their campaign efforts. They got together on Election Day an anxiously waited to learn the outcome.

It was a long night but worth it because their candidate made it to the State Senate!

When the jumping, clapping and hugging were over, a young girl wondered if the work was done. Helene answered that it had, on the contrary, just started and that they would continue to meet to support the candidate's work and especially to make sure he kept his word. They agreed to take a short vacation and to meet in a week.

A couple of days later, Helene received a call from Martin, Rhoda's friend, who wanted to know if she had had any more suspicious note. She had not, and had also forgotten all about it but Martin advised her to be on the alert because there were some violent groups waiting for opportunities to attack and to create social turmoil. Helene found it hard to believe so Martin added that unfortunately not everybody was as honest and warmhearted as she was.

During those days she had got back in contact with Martin and with the owners of the South American coffee shop so they planned a meeting to share experiences and to debate about educational high school opportunities and discrimination.

They met at the coffee shop after it had closed to the public. It was just a small group of people concerned about the future of their children. Helene had told the "Evening Review" editor about it and was hoping he would also attend the meeting.

It was a peaceful one where some of them shared their bad experiences. Helene stood up to start telling them about their rights and to suggest different possible actions when there was a loud knock at the door. It was the police who stormed in, arrested Helene, chased the rest away and took her to the police station. When they were leaving, she heard a familiar click and saw a flash. She did not need to ask who it was and thought, "Well . . . the Evening Review did come in the end!" Once at the police station she was informed that she had been accused of taking advantage of young people and trying to manipulate them to make them follow her desires. She was sent to a cell while Rhoda desperately called Martin.

Rhoda visited her the next day and told her that she had been accused by the mother of one of the young students she had been tutoring and that the lady was making every possible effort to keep her in jail. It was not so easy for Martin to set her free this time; Helene was taken to Court where she had to endure the lady's nasty comments on her personality.

Court was crowded and the press was there, only this time it did not make her happy at all.

There was a small crowd outside Court: Helene's friends who were demanding to have her released.

After listening to the young student's deposition and taking into account that he was of legal age and fairly educated, the judge decided there was not enough evidence for a trial but still reminded Helene that they were going through special shaky times; that age difference did matter and that even if she had the right to speak her mind ,she should choose her interlocutors more carefully and avoid situations such as the present one. They young boy's mother started complaining so she was escorted out of Court.

The public clapped and congratulated Helene but she did not feel happy: in her opinion she had been unfairly blamed and lectured.

When she was getting in her car she heard another click. She angrily turned around but could see nobody.

Later that day Rhoda paid her a visit and smiling showed her the paper: there was her picture on it with a caption that read: "Justice prevails." Unfortunately it was not enough to cheer her up. In her opinion her life had been ruined and in a way she was right because the worst was yet to come.

As a consequence of this incident, she was fired from the library because they did not want to run any risks by having her.

Rhoda tried her best to help her out and proved to be one of her best friends. Because of her organizational skills and contacts she was able to find lecture opportunities for Helene who could make a decent living by attending different events and sharing her life experience. Helene felt very grateful to Rhoda and when she decided to write another autobiography she mentioned her and praised her by saying: "When New York City went bankrupt, its Department of Civil Affairs and Public Events was closed down and all the duties formerly shared by several executives devolved upon one small Assistant to the Mayor, still in her thirties, Rhoda Martin. At almost no cost to the City of New York Rhoda managed to create city-wide celebrations by enlisting the city's various working communities into a workforce to brighten the lives of New Yorkers all year round. Her awesome talents in the performance of these duties and her selfless devotion to the City of New York are equaled only by her talent for selfless and devoted friendship"

That friendship kept on growing and would last for over 40 years; a lot longer than Helene's books at the publishers because, once again, her autobiographical works proved to be a failure. Helene was very good at doing research and writing history books but terrible when writing about her own life. For some reason, when she wrote about herself she left passion aside so the whole product looked like some sort of biographical report not many people would be interested in reading.

Many years had gone by and important changes had taken place thanks to the efforts of many reformers. Helene was happy to have been part of those changes and always remembered her former friends. Colleges had become the center of research and debate, which pleased Helene, who had always been a great supporter of education. One of the things that pleased her the most was to see Martina's children attending college and not being discriminated any more.

Of the most common topics of debate in those times were war and the mandatory draft. Most college students were against them and there had been unpleasant confrontations concerning them.

In September 1969, Helene was commissioned to write a book on the young reformers of the sixties. In order to do the necessary research, she started visiting the University of Columbia whose library she thoroughly enjoyed. She was also enjoying working on her new book called "Here and Now "because it would deal with recent history and issues of national interest.

One day she had been working hard on her research, completely unaware of what was going on around her. The students had held a demonstration on campus and organized a sitting down. They had been asked to leave the premises but had refused to do so.

As Helene was walking out of the library, she noticed many students sitting on the grass, talking or simply reading. The weather was nice so she decided to do the same and relax for a while.

It was then when it happened: the police cars, the running and yelling and once again her being thrown into a police van.

As Helene was the oldest, she had to tolerate funny gazes and whispering so she was truly glad when they were all released a few hours later. She smiled to herself remembering the times when Rhoda and Martin had come to her rescue and the passion they had applied to her defense. War had become the main focus of interest ,there were demonstrations against it almost every day but this time Helene did not take part in them, she continued to work on her book and to dream about being a successful writer.

When she was done, she took it to the publisher she knew: no interest . . . again. She was unemployed . . . again!

Helene sighed and considered her possibilities which, at her age, were not too many.

Then she smiled: she would soon find a way out, she had done so before; she just needed a new plan of action . . . again.

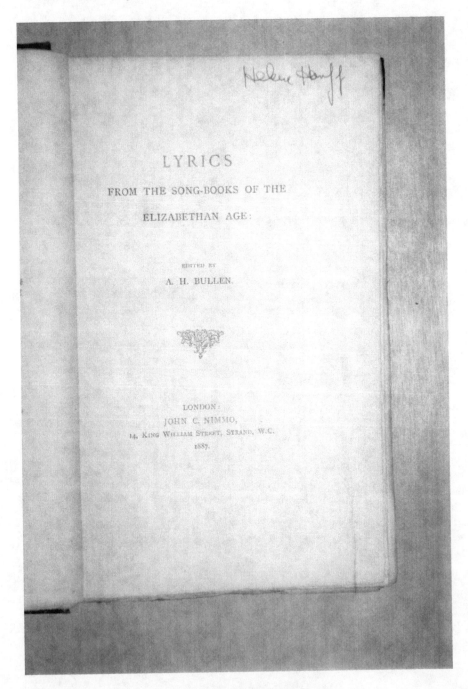

A Book of Elizabethan Love Poems

CHAPTER 13

As a lifelong resident of New York City, Helene had always enjoyed the busy urban scene. She loved to attend cultural events and dine out with friends, to walk through Central Park on a warm spring day, and to become part of the throng of busy Fifth Avenue shoppers. She lived in a small rent controlled apartment and was a fixture at a local neighborhood bar named Eddie's Place, where she spent a couple of evenings each week perched on a bar stool, smoking one cigarette after another, laughing and chatting with friends and acquaintances. She was a local celebrity of sorts, the author of a series of literary detective novels. She had a small loyal following of readers, many of whom made a habit of dropping into Eddie's to see her.

The oldest bartender at Eddie's was a special friend of hers. Jack Thompson was one of those rough on the exterior but tenderhearted characters that New York is famous for. Jack always cleared her favorite stool at the corner of the bar as soon as she walked through the door and knew exactly how to fix her martini. All in all, life in New York was good for Helene. She rarely regretted her decision never to marry or have children. Between her work and friends, she lived a full and busy life. Her close friend Harriet, a magazine writer, had also never married. Their friendship had endured through the years and they had come to depend upon each other. The shared each other's joys and successes and were there for each other in times of stress. Helene and Harriet used to say that their writing had taken the place of children, allowing them to satisfy the urge to create something without enduring the hardship and responsibility of motherhood.

Helene showed no signs of slowing down until she reached her mid-seventies, when she began to spend more time in her apartment. She seemed to have lost interest in theater performances and concerts, venturing out only for an occasional meal with friends. The truth was she was becoming increasingly forgetful. Her memory had always been a source of pride—she was famous among her friends for remembering details about experiences from decades before. Now names and faces from the past and present were often a jumble and she couldn't decide whether an event she remembered had taken place in a book she had read or in her own life. Years of heavy drinking and chain smoking had taken its toll. Although her friend Harriet was only two years younger, Helene's health problems and memory loss made her seem a decade older.

In the winter of 1992, Helene's visits to Eddie's Place became less frequent. As time passed, fewer of her drinking buddies asked her bartender friend Jack where she was. But Jack didn't forget about Helene and would call her apartment to find how she was doing if he hadn't seen her in a couple of weeks. Then she would make the effort to dress up a little and spend an evening on her favorite stool at Eddie's, where for at least an evening she could drink her martinis and turn back the hands of time.

In her younger years, Helene often wished she could settle down and devote more time to her work. Now she was spending more time at home, but she found it difficult to write. She was unable to concentrate and keep her thoughts straight. Finally she had to put aside her latest book project. Even her reading was affected. She was no longer able to focus on the history books she loved and began to limit her reading to *The New York Times*. She spent an increasing amount of time listening to talk radio and the news, trying to make sense out of a world that seemed to be passing her by.

Helene began to see the value in having children who could have helped her keep things organized. Her once neat apartment had become cluttered. Rather than paying bills immediately and then filing them away as had been her habit, she let piles of mail accumulate. Every now and then she would experience a burst of housekeeping zeal, stuffing piles of newspapers and bills into plastic shopping bags which she then piled into a closet or shoved under her bed. Bills weren't being paid and creditors began to call the apartment. Most were happy to take Helene's credit card number when she offered it as payment, but she was only compounding her problems since she wasn't taking care of her credit card bills.

A few years earlier, Helene had been diagnosed with Type 2 Diabetes. She had made a habit of checking her blood sugar level and taking her medication, but she had never been very good about balancing her diet. Now she was forgetting to order groceries, though she always seemed to remember to have liquor and cigarettes delivered from the local liquor store. Her closest friends worried that she wasn't taking care of herself and started to wonder how long she could continue to live by herself in her apartment. Harriet stopped by every few days and observed Helene's deteriorating health with concern. Finally she insisted that Helene get a complete medical checkup.

Dr. Adams, Helene's long-time physician, had retired several years before and turned over his practice to a Dr. Goldstone. Helene had never felt as comfortable with Dr. Goldstone as she had with Dr. Adams, probably because he was only half her age. Now her diabetes symptoms had worsened and she often felt fatigued, dizzy and nauseated. Harriet made an appointment for Helene with Dr. Goldstone. The morning of the appointment Harriet arrived at Helene's apartment and helped her get dressed, then took her downstairs and found a cab. Harriet didn't want to take any chances with Helene missing her appointment or getting confused about her symptoms, so she stayed with her in the waiting room and sat in during the examination.

Dr. Goldstone adjusted Helene's medication and gave her a serious talking to about her dietary habits. He impressed upon her the need to eat a balanced diet, to increase her level of activity, and to cut down on smoking and drinking. Harriet mentioned Helene's memory problems, but Dr. Goldstone suggested that could be a symptom of her diabetes. He said her memory lapses might clear up when she began to take better care of herself. Helene was attentive during his instructions and on the way home from his office she promised Harriet that she would pay more attention to her diet and cut down on cigarettes and drinking.

Things were better with Helene for a few weeks thanks in large part to Harriet making an extra effort to visit more often. Harriet made sure she was buying groceries and eating according to her prescribed diet. As summer approached, Harriet began to worry about leaving Helene alone while she made a long-anticipated trip to visit family and friends in California. She called Helene's brother Arthur, who lived in Vermont. Arthur volunteered his daughter Connie as a stand-in for Harriet. Connie had recently graduated from Bennington College with a degree in International Relations and was beginning an internship at the United Nations Headquarters in New York. It was agreed that Connie would check in on Helene, run errands as needed and make sure she was watching her diet.

Summer began and Harriet left for her West Coast visit, feeling somewhat at ease about Helene's situation. Things started out well with Connie, who devoted a couple of weekends to cleaning up Helene's apartment, sorting through her paperwork and getting her finances in control. She was surprised to find that Helene has accumulated several thousand dollars in credit card debt over the past few months. She had apparently given her credit card number to some telemarketers, thinking they were bill collectors. Helene had a small income from book royalties as well as some savings, but Connie didn't want to wipe out her aunt's savings to pay off her credit cards. Instead, she set up a payment plan that would eliminate the debt over time. She was unsuccessful when she tried to get Helene to give up her cards. Helene was steadfast about holding on to her credit cards, seeing them as one of the last symbols of her independence.

Connie had the best of intentions when it came to her aunt, but her internship turned out to be more demanding than she had expected. She was unable to check in on Helene as often as she should have. Helene, feeling deserted by both Harriet and Connie, reverted to her old bad habits. The Olympic Games were being televised and she spent hours in front of the television, drinking vodka and smoking one cigarette after another. She ignored an irritating cough until she woke up one morning with a high fever and blinding headache. She tossed and turned for three days as her fever repeatedly rose and then broke, leaving her drenched in sweat. Finally she began to feel better and her headache subsided, but the cough remained and she was so weak that she could only get out of bed for a few hours each day.

After only a couple of weeks Helene again began to feel a fever coming on again. This time she suffered through it for only one day before calling Connie, who rushed over and found Helene barely able to answer the door. In the emergency room a couple of hours later, Helene was diagnosed with pneumonia. Her diabetes left her especially vulnerable to infection, so she was checked into the hospital and treated with strong antibiotics. Harriet returned from her trip the day after Helene was released from the hospital and was disappointed to find her friend in such a weakened state.

After returning from the hospital Helene was almost completely confined to her apartment. Harriet contacted many of Helene's old friends who took turns visiting and bringing her food items to tempt her diminished appetite. Helene's formerly buxom figure was just a memory since she had lost a considerable amount of weight and taken on a frail appearance. Although her spirits were good and she did her best to entertain visitors, her memory loss had returned. Dr. Goldstone was concerned about her blood sugar levels and had begun to wonder if Helene would soon need daily insulin shots. In the fall, Helene caught pneumonia and was hospitalized for a third time. This time, she was critically ill and was admitted to the intensive care unit. One night she was very near death, but she rallied. When she awoke the next morning she was greeted by the relieved faces of Harriet and her brother Arthur Exhausted, she finally had to admit that she was unable to live alone and take care of herself. When she was ready to leave the hospital a week later, she agreed to enter a nursing home "on a temporary basis." On October 3, 1996, she was moved to the DeWitt Nursing Home in New York.

Harriet and Arthur had done their homework and found what they hoped was the best possible facility for Helene. DeWitt was located a few blocks from her apartment. It was sunny and clean, with a friendly staff that provided a full roster of activities to help keep residents engaged with life. DeWitt was a single story, square building with a courtyard at its center. A single hallway ran along each side of the square, with residents' rooms and public rooms off each side of the hall. Most residents were assigned two to a room, though there were a few private rooms. Posters and paintings were hung in the hallways and public rooms and residents were encouraged to decorate their own rooms. Fresh flowers brightened the front reception area and nurses stations. Most of the residents of the nursing home were people like Helene who were dealing with the effects of aging. There was also a smattering of younger residents, most of who were recovering from serious illnesses or injuries. A few residents had been paralyzed or disabled by stroke and were facing permanent residency in the nursing home.

Helene's first few days at DeWitt didn't seem very different from the hospital. She slept a lot, picked at the meals that were placed before her, and was helped out of bed to visit the restroom. As she began to regain her strength, she was encouraged to do more things for herself. A new physician, Dr. Rao, looked in on her every day. After a week he encouraged her to start using a walker and to take her meals in the public dining room. One of the nurses brought her a calendar of activities and a pen, asking her to circle the ones she wanted to participate in. Bingo, movies, current event lectures and even book discussions were available, but Helene didn't feel up to getting involved.

As the days passed and she became stronger, she missed her independence. Having spent most of her adult life living alone, she was having a hard time adjusting to the constant presence of other people at the nursing home. Her roommate was a Chinese woman in her nineties who kept to herself, but Helene still felt her presence as an invasion of privacy. Although she was surrounded by people, she felt very alone. She longed to return to her apartment but knew she had done a poor job of taking care of herself. During this period, attendants and nurses at DeWitt came to know her as a feisty character and flinty old soul who was determined to get well enough to return to her apartment.

While Helene was living at DeWitt Nursing Home, her friend Harriet and her niece Connie became her essential lifelines to the outside world.

They visited her weekly and were happy to bring her anything she asked for. She called them often, asking them to check on her apartment and run errands for her. One day Harriet received 49 calls from Helene, who was worried about paying her rent and other bills. Harriet assured her that everything would be taken care of, though she had serious doubts. Connie had told her everything about the state of Helene's finances. Harriet wondered whether Helene would ever be able to return to her apartment and how long they should keep dipping into her savings to pay the rent and credit card bills.

The nurses and orderlies at DeWitt Nursing Home were mostly Filipino. Although they were unfailingly polite, many found their kindnesses met with a stony silence or a curt reply from Helene. They assumed she was prejudiced, but Helene's reaction to them wasn't related to the fact that they were Filipino. She had been a supporter of civil rights since the 1960s and would have been surprised to hear accusations of racism. The truth was that Helene resented their youth and energy. As her medical report revealed, this was one of the symptoms of senile dementia. Helene's brain was dying faster than her body, but both were victims of decades of tobacco and alcohol and a sedentary lifestyle. Ironically, one of her most endearing characteristics, her love of her apartment and the inner life of reading were both enemies to her cardio-vascular system. Every time she looked at their trim figures and smooth skin, she was reminded that her youth was long gone. For the first time in her life, she was feeling the limitations of her age. Time was now her enemy.

As the weeks and months passed, Helene gradually became more comfortable at DeWitt. She began to participate in scheduled activities. After getting to know the staff members, she grew to like and respect them as people. She came to the realization that this was their time to be young and she stopped envying them for their youth. She appreciated their efforts to make life more pleasant for the nursing home residents. Helene formed special relationships with two of the workers at DeWitt. One was Juliet, a small, capable woman who supervised the nurses' station at night. When Helene had a hard time sleeping, she and Juliet would sneak out to the patio off the dining room to smoke. Juliet was a widow with three children who were attending college in the Philippines. She shared a small apartment with two other nurses and sent a large portion of her salary to her children. In return, she expected them to study hard and join her in the U.S. when they had completed their degrees. Another of Helene's favorite nursing home workers was Victor. He was also from the Philippines, but was in his early twenties and single. Handsome and funny, he was popular among the young staff members at DeWitt. He had a special gift for bringing out the best in the residents of the nursing home. He was often called upon to complete the most unpleasant duties, but he was never seen without a smile on his face. Victor was the first person to break through Helene's shell and help her adjust to her new life in the nursing home.

Over time, Helene began to come to terms with her advancing age. At her doctor's suggestion, she asked Harriet to bring photos from her apartment and she used them to decorate the walls of her room. She loved to talk about the people in the photos to anyone who would listen. There were pictures from her childhood, pictures of Arthur's family, pictures of friends from Eddie's Place and even some pictures of well-known authors that she had known and admired over the years. The photos helped her memory, which had greatly improved now that alcohol was no longer available.

As she began to feel more like her old self, Helene took more interest in the other DeWitt residents and enjoying hearing about their life histories. Her writer's curiosity had never left her and she was always interested in the forces that had shaped the lives of the people she met. She still had days of forgetfulness, but on her best days she was a welcome presence in the dining room and other public areas of the nursing home. Helene became especially close with another resident named Tony Walsh, who was a few years older than Helene and recovering from a stroke that had left him partially paralyzed and unable to speak. In the two years that Tony had been a patient at DeWitt, his condition had vastly improved. His paralysis had lessened and he was able to walk on his own. His left arm was still immobile, but he had learned to compensate. His once-slurred speech was now easy to understand and his conversations showed evidence of a quick and well-disciplined mind.

Helene and Tony gravitated to each other because they were kindred spirits, two New York natives who had been toughened by life in the city. Tony told Helene that she reminded him of a girl from his old neighborhood named Kitty. This girl grew up tough, able to hold her own against any kid on a block full of tough kids. Kitty had gone on to become a tough-as-nails lawyer working in the district attorney's office. Tony sometimes called Helene by the name Kitty, leading the nurses and orderlies to think that he was confusing her with someone else. Sometimes Helene wondered herself. Between his lapses in memory and her own, it wasn't unusual for their conversations to take a strange turn.

Not long after they became friends, Tony and Helene were constant companions. Tony had once been married and had a son named John who visited him a couple of times a month. He never spoke about his wife, but he was clearly proud of his son, a tall, handsome middle-aged man who looked like he spent a lot of time outdoors. Although Tony was now somewhat stooped, it was obvious that he also had once been tall, muscular and handsome. He carried himself with dignity and retained the charm of a man who had a way with women. Tony was attentive to Helene in a way that was more than flattering. He put her so much at ease that she often felt as if they had been friends for years. They had inside jokes about the other patients and the staff at DeWitt and always seemed to be conspiring about something.

In fact, sometimes Tony and Helene actually were conspiring. One day after Helene had been at DeWitt for about six months, Tony confided in her his plans for "The Great Escape." During the time he was recovering from his stroke, he had never left DeWitt unaccompanied by nursing home staff. The patients were sometimes taken on outings or shopping trips, where they were always supervised by orderlies or nurses. Now that Tony was beginning to feel better, he was eager for a field trip on his own. He asked Helene join him on his outing. She went along with his planning, doubting that anything would ever come of it. Tony didn't talk too much about his past, but he did like to reminisce about a house named Fox Hollow that had been very important to him. It was located somewhere near water and included landscaped grounds. Helene assumed it was a place from his childhood. The house figured largely in his plans for The Great Escape.

One Friday morning in May Tony told Helene the plans were all set for the following day. Although she had never really been sure if he was serious about getting away from DeWitt, it now was apparent that he was very serious. He took her aside while most of the residents were involved in a bingo tournament, showed her a set of car keys and told her to pack a bag. Her initial shock gave way to excitement as she felt a long-dormant sense of adventure reawakening. The plan was to leave right after breakfast on Saturday. There were fewer staff members on duty over the weekend and with visitors going in and out it would be several hours before they were missed.

The following morning Helene could barely contain her excitement. The night before she had packed a shopping bag with a change of clothing and a few personal items and stashed it under her bed. After breakfast, she retrieved the bag, put her medication into her purse and set off to meet Tony at the back door of the nursing home. She had a sinking feeling when she turned the corner of the hall and saw Victor waiting with Tony, but the smile on Tony's face told her everything must be going according to plan. Victor opened the nursing home door and escorted them out to the parking lot. They stopped in front of a blue convertible VW. As Victor gave them a few operating instructions, Helene realized it must be his car. Then Tony slid in behind the wheel and Victor helped Helene into the front passenger seat, giving her a wink as he closed the door. Victor reminded Tony that he had promised to return by Sunday evening, then waved goodbye as Tony started the car and they headed out of the parking lot.

With a roar of the engine, Tony joined the stream of traffic. The VW had a stick shift and Tony experimented with trying to steady the wheel with his disabled left arm while he used his right hand to shift. This wasn't really working so he asked Helene to try shifting while he operated the clutch. They had much more success with this and it made them feel like a team. Tony knew exactly where he was going and before too long they were entering the Queens-Midtown Tunnel, heading towards Long Island. The day was sunny and warm and the traffic was heavy, but Tony and Helene were enjoying their freedom too much to mind waiting in traffic. It had been years since Helene had ridden in a convertible and she savored the feeling of the wind in her hair. They found a radio station that was playing big band music and sang along to the songs from their youth.

After they passed through Queens the traffic began to thin and soon they were in the Hamptons. In her younger days, Helene had summered a few times in the East Hampton with friends, but it had been decades since her last visit. She convinced Tony to stop at a small seafood restaurant where she used one of her credit cards to buy lunch. She even indulged herself with a martini in celebration of their newfound freedom. Tony said he had never been a drinker, but he raised his glass of water and they toasted The Great Escape. After lunch they parked near a small beach and walked along the sand. Helene kicked off her shoes and waded in the waves while Tony watched from his perch on top of a sand dune. She could have stayed all afternoon, but Tony was eager to get back on the road. His mind seemed clear and he definitely had a destination in mind, but Helene couldn't get much information out of him. She didn't press him too hard and concentrated instead on enjoying each minute of the day.

After leaving the beach, they drove along Montauk Highway and into the village of Watermill. They stopped and bought groceries for a picnic dinner: bread, salami, cheese, apples and wine. A few miles outside of Watermill, Tony left the highway and drove along a smaller road that skirted the eastern shore of Mecox Bay. The sun glinted on the water and a gentle breeze filled the sails of boats that were out on the bay. On each side of the road, large homes could be glimpsed at the end of long drives. Tony started to slow the VW and asked Helene to downshift. He turned onto a side road and they passed through a small stand of trees. They were surrounded by beautifully landscaped grounds. Another turn in the road revealed a wide expanse of lawn rolling up to a stately home. The two-story mansion was white with black shutters and a red roof. Tall white columns flanked an entryway which was dominated by a large black door.

Helene looked at Tony in surprise. This must be the house that he had described so often to her back at DeWitt. She recognized many features he had mentioned, including the rose garden to the right of the front door. Tony followed the driveway around to the side of the house and parked in front of a large garage that was designed in the same style as the house. He helped Helene out of the car and led her on a tour of the gardens that encircled the house, pointing out special plants and flowers. He knew this place so well that Helene began to wonder if he was the owner. Ever the author looking for a story, she refrained from asking him too many questions and instead let him do most of the talking.

After Tony had shown Helene the gardens he led her down to the bay, where a small beach and dock provided access to the water. They watched the sailboats, savoring the beauty that surrounded them. As they walked backed to the VW, Helene assumed they would get in the car and drive away. Instead, Tony reached into the backseat and took out her overnight bag and his own small duffle bag. He handed her the bag of groceries they had purchased in the village, then led her back towards the mansion, stopping in front of a door at the back of the house. An urn with trailing ivy stood next to the door. The ivy was in a pot, which Tony lifted and reached under. He pulled out a key and used it to open the door. Helene half expected to hear an alarm go off, but nothing disturbed the peaceful silence. Beckoning Helene to follow, Tony walked into the house as if he were returning home from a long vacation.

The interior of the house did not disappoint. Room after room was decorated with understated but exquisite taste. Helene later told Harriet how they had eaten their picnic dinner on the veranda and watched the sun set into the bay. They spent the night in one of the guest rooms and finished the remainder of their picnic food for breakfast. As they ate,

Tony told Helene about his connection to the house. He had lived there for thirty years as groundskeeper, and most of the gardens and landscaping were his creation. The owner of the house was a retired financier who spent several months each year in Italy. After Tony's stroke, his son John had taken over as groundskeeper. John had hidden the key in the urn and disarmed the house's alarm system, then spent the weekend with a girl friend in Watermill.

Late in the morning, Tony and Helene made one last tour of Fox Hollow to make sure everything was in order. He locked the door and replaced the key in the urn, and then they loaded their bags into the Volkswagen and started their trip back to the city. At Tony's request, they stopped for pizza at a small café in Queens. They made it back to DeWitt in time for dinner, where Tony returned the VW to the back parking lot. They went in through the front door and endured questions and admonishments from the nursing home staff. The shared adventure brought Tony and Helene closer and they conducted themselves like a couple who had been together for years. They never revealed details of their weekend to any of the staff, though Helene did confide in Harriet. The Great Escape went on to become something of a legend at DeWitt Nursing Home, a story that persisted even years after Tony had recovered sufficiently from his stroke to return to Fox Hollow, where he worked alongside his son John as assistant groundskeeper until his death.

Helene would retain the memory of her weekend adventure even when she had trouble remembering more important events in her life. It would be her final visit to the Hamptons but not her last adventure.

It was just past 11AM on an unusually cold April day. It was hard to believe that Spring had arrived three weeks before as the gray clouds scudded across the sky and only small bits of deep blue shown here and there. The wind had scattered ribbons, flags and plastic flowers that had been left on other graves. The officiating rabbi's voice drifted softly in the window and the few mourners huddled with shoulders hunched and collars pulled up to fight off the cold. As the coffin was lowered I thought of the quotation from John Donne that Helene had spoken in the movie, that men's souls were all books in God's library. I thought how perfect this was for Helene for if she had been a practicing Buddhist, there is little doubt that either in a past life or a future one, she would be a book. And not just any book, but a book about someone who had lived long ago and had witnessed great events in the history of England. This was what most thrilled Helene: a view from her window in her bed-sitter apartment of New York's East Side of Richard III or Charles II or Thomas Beckett as he waited in Canterbury for his assassins. Helene would have wanted no more than that, to see from a safe distance the great events that shaped the nation she loved. Somehow, I think most of us hope that the spirit of Helene Hanff has found a resting place, not in a grave in New York City, but a pastoral place in England's green land, bright, beautiful and full of wonder.

A few weeks after the funeral, Rhoda came out to visit the grave. She wanted to give her friend a bouquet of roses. There had been so many people at Helene's funeral, it had been hard to get close to the grave.

As she mused over her friend's headstone—the headstone she had paid for—Rhoda fought down a feeling that perhaps in this friendship she had given more than she had received. Not that Helene wasn't a great friend—she was. But Rhoda had felt a caretaker sometimes, getting Helene jobs, keeping Helene supported, shielding Helene's pride, gently steering Helene away from the sharp words and sarcastic nature that had caused her to run the Democratic Club with an iron fist, paying for things. Rhoda knew she had a salutary effect on Helene's life, and she was glad of it, but she was weary too. She'd taken care of her mother and now Helene for quite a few years.

She was startled by footsteps in the cemetery. It was an overcast day, the place was deserted, and she felt a little fear as she saw a man enter the gates, look around, and then approach the area where she was at. She relaxed a little when she saw he was not young and something of a fussy, professorial type—tweedy, intellectual, and harmless. Then she knew.

"Tom?" she quavered.

"Rhoda?" He was at her side in an instant. "I read about it in the newspapers she sent me. She gave me a subscription. Funny thing for her to do—I always thought of Helene as being a little on the harsh side, for all her idealism. It seemed like such a thoughtful thing to do."

"Oh, she was thoughtful," Rhoda cried. "She was a great, great, great friend!"

"Maybe that's just your own kindness speaking, Rhoda. You are one of the kindest people I have ever met. I've never stopped thinking so."

They decided to go for coffee in the charming little rural town to renew their acquaintance. Their eyes were glowing with excitement at their reunion.

Rhoda turned for one last look at Helene's headstone before leaving the cemetery arm-in-arm with Tom.

"Thank you," she whispered to her friend.

Without realizing it, Helene had become a larger part of my life than I had thought. I had grown accustomed to the idea of her death the minute I found out she had been placed in a nursing home; people do not go home after that. It is, as they say, God's waiting room. As I said, though, I had grown accustomed to the idea of her dying but not its reality. The sun had broken through the clouds and I thought that it was not fair, that a person who had given so much to so many deserved a steady rain on the city she loved. I hailed a cab, but instead of going home, I went to her apartment on 72nd Street. It would be a farewell to not only Helene but to a big part of my life, a part that was filled with intellectual curiosity and the heart of a rally good person.

As I approached and paid the cabbie, a station wagon was parked at the door with an elderly woman sitting in the passenger seat. I wouldn't give it a second thought; she was guarding the car against the meter maids. But the tailgate was open and inside the storage compartment I recognized a familiar object. It was a poster from 84 Charing Cross Road: The Movie. It had been blown open by the wind as it had been placed on six or seven smallish boxes, what are called in the moving trade, "book boxes."

I used the key Helene gave me fully planning on leaving it in the apartment. The eighth floor was much the way it always was. Helene's door, however, was propped slightly open with a half-packed box of knick-knacks. I paused outside and heard two women talking.

"My God, this place smells like a goddamned ashtray. We'll never get the smell out. I knew she wasn't the cleanest person in the family but the filth. Oy Vey. And I am NOT going to clean out the refrigerator."

"It's probably full of gin bottles. Let's see."

I heard the fridge door open.

"See, I told you. Wonder bread and gin. A very good diet. She committed suicide on this dreck."

"Let's get the rest of this packed. My stomach is turning."

I gently knocked with my knuckle. Two older women, well-dressed in a conservative New York City kind of way, answered the door.

"Can we help you?" one asked.

"Oh, I'm looking for . . . " I stumbled.

"Looking for who?" she asked putting her hand on her hip and raising her voice just enough to indicate she was being bothered.

"Arthur. Uh, Arthur Quiller-Couch," I said stupidly.

"Well, dearie, with a name like that, I would think he lived in London, not New York," she smiled.

"I must be on the wrong floor. Beg your pardon."

The door closed in my face but I didn't stay to listen.

Epilogue

I have reprinted below with some emendations from my last printing, books in the library of Helene Hanff. What they say about her is up to the reader to discern and I cannot vouch for any ideas as to which books she read and which she just kept waiting to read or never planning to read. Helene had her complexities, many of which arise from the anonymity of her life. Very little of consequence was ever written and it was not until the 1970s that anyone thought to write anything and most of it is shallow and, in some respects, maudlin insofar as writers about her tended to idolize her and truth and accuracy are not the province of idolaters.

84, Charring Cross Road, first edition

The Library of Helene Hanff

1. Abbott, Jeffrey. **The Only Good Yankee**. New York: Ballantine Books, 1995.

2. Allen, Woody. **Getting Even**. New York: Random House, 1978.

3. American Red Cross. **Standard First Aid and Personal Safety.** Garden City: Doubleday & Co., 1977.

4. **The American Heritage Dictionary of the English Language**. Boston: Houghton Mifflin Co., 1975.

5. **Anthology for the Enjoyment of Poetry**. Eastman, Max, ed. New York: Charles Scribners' Sons, 1939.

6. **An Anthology of Light Verse**. Kronenberg, Louis, ed. New York: The Modern Library, 1935.

7. Antin, Francois. **Mots D'Heures**. New York: Grossman Publishers, 1967.

8. **Selections from Aristotle**. Loomis, Louise, ed. New York: Walter J. Black, 1943.

9. Arnold Matthew. **The Function of Criticism at the Present Time**. New York: The Macmillan Co., 1900.

10. **Selections from the Prose Works of Matthew Arnold**. Johnson, William Savage, ed. Boston: Houghton Mifflin Co., 1913.

11. Aubrey, John. **Brief Lives and Other Selected Writings**. London: The Cresset Press, 1949.

12. Austen, Jane. **Emma**. Illustrated by Philip Gough. London: Macdonald & Co., 1950.

13. Austen, Jane. **Mansfield Park**. London: J.M. Dent & Sons, Ltd., 1951.

14. Austen, Jane. **Northanger Abbey**. Illustrated by Robert Austin. Introduction by V.S. Pritchett. London: Avalon Prss, 1948.

15. Austen, Jane. **Persuasion**. London: The Book Society, 1944.

16. Austen, Jane. **Pride and Prejudice**. London: Avalon Press, 1949.

17. Austen, Jane. **Pride and Prejudice**. London: Collins Publishing, 1966.

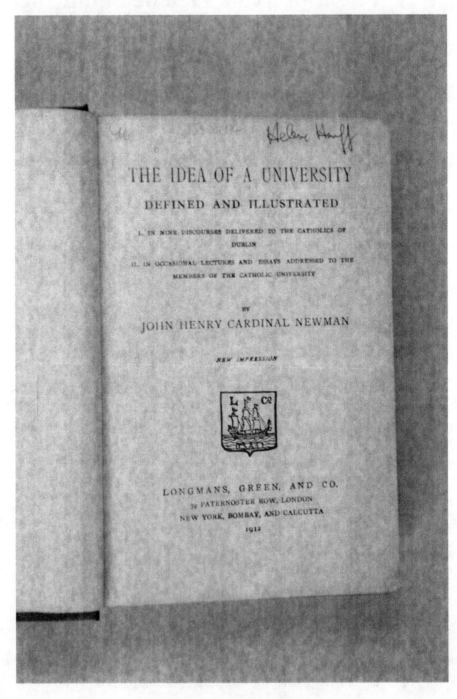

Newman's Idea of a University

18. Bach, Johanna Sebastian. **The Passion of Our Lord According to St. Matthew**. London: Novello & Co., 1948.

19. Bacon, Francis. **Essays and Colours of Good and Evil**. London: The Macmillan Co., 1903

20. Bacon, Francis. **The New Atlantis**. New York: Walter J. Black, 1942.

21. Baldwin, James. **Notes of a Native Son**. Boston: The Beacon Press, 1955.

22. Baldwin, James. **The Price of the Ticket: Collected Non-Fiction**, 1948-1985. New York: St. Martin's Press, 1985.

23. Barnard, Robert. **Corpse in a Gilded Cage**. New York: Dell Publishing, 1988.

24. Barnes, Julian. **Letters from London**, 1990-1995. London: Picador Publishing, 1995.

25. Beckham, Rex. **Lit a la Carte: Favorite Recipes of Famous Authors**. Soquel: Bay Side Press, 1995. Contained Hanff's recipe for "Deviled Crabs."

26. Bennett, Charles E. **New Latin Grammar**. Boston: Allyn & Bacon, 1924.

27. Bernstein, Theodore M. **Bernstein's Reserve Dictionary**. New York: Times Books, 1977.

28. Bettelheim, Bruno. **The Uses of Enchantment: The Meaning and Importance of Fairy Tales**. New York: Random House, 1977.

29. Bible. **New Testament in Greek**. London: British and Foreign Bible Society, 1913.

30. **Bible. English. Authorized. Containing the Old and New Testaments and the Apocrypha**. Three volumes. London: The Grolier Society, [n.d.]

31. **Bible. Old Testament**. English. **The Holy Scriptures According to the Masoretic Text**. Philadelphia: The Jewish Publication Society of America, 1928. Presentation Bookplate to Helene Hanff, May 22, 1931.

32. **Bible. New Testament**. Latin. Beroline: Sumptibus Societa-

tus Bibliophilorum Britannicae et Externae, 1911.

33. **Bible. New Testament.** Latin. Londini: Henricum Frowde, 1911.

34. Bierman, June. **The Diabetic's Total Health Book.** New York: Pocket Books, 1982.

35. Black, Mary. **Old New York in Early Photographs, 1853 -1901.** New York: Dover Publications, 1976.

36. Blom, Benjamin. **People Mostly: New York in Photographs** 1900 – 1950. New York: The Amayllis Press, 1983.

37. Boleslavsky, Richard. **Acting: The First Six Lessons.** New York: Theatre Arts Books, 1949.

38. **Book Lovers' Quotations.** Helen Exley, ed. London: Watford: Exley Publishing, 1991.

39. **The Book of Musical Anecdotes.** Norman Lebrecht, ed. London: Andre Deutsch, 1985.

40. **The Book of Sonnet Sequences.** Howard Peterson, ed. London: Longmans, Green & Co., 1930.

41. **The Book-Lovers' Anthology.** R.M. Leonard, ed. London: Henry Frowde, 1911.

42. Boswell, James. **The Life of Samuel Johnson, LL.D.** London: J.M.Dent & Co., 1909-1911. 2 Vol.

43. **The Brand – X Anthology of Poetry.** William Zaranka, ed. Cambridge: Apple-Wood Books, 1981.

44. Brittain, F. Arthur Quiller-Couch: **A Biographical Study of Q.** Cambridge: University Press, 1948. 2 cc. One inscribed to Helene Hanff from Muriel Brittain.

45. Brodsky, Jack. **The Cleopatra Papers: A Private Correspondence.** New York: Simon & Schuster, 1963.

46. Brown, Ivor. **Jane Austen and Her World.** New York: Henry Z. Walck, 1966.

47. Brown, Richard. **The London Bookshop.** Pinner: Private Libraries Association, 1922. 2 vols, only the second volume being here present.

48. Browne, Sir Thomas. **The Religio Medici and Other Writings**. London: J.M. Dent & Sons, Ltd., 1945.

49. Browning, Elizabeth Barrett. **Sonnets from the Portuguese**. London: T.C. & E.C. Jack, n.d.

50. Browing, Elizabeth Barrett. **Sonnets from the Portuguese**. New York: The Heritage Press, 1948.

51. Browning, Robert. **The Courtship Correspondence 1845 – 1846**. Oxford: The University Press, 1990.

52. Browning, Robert. **Men and Women**. London: J.M. Dent & Co.,1899.

53. Browning, Robert. **Poems**. New York: Walter J. Black, 1932.

54. Bryant, Arthur. **The Lion and the Unicorn: A Historian's Testament**. Garden City: Doubleday & Co., 1970.

55. Bullock, Helen. **My Head and My Heart: A Little History of Thomas Jefferson and Maria Cosway**. New York: G.P. Putnam's Sons, 1945.

56. Burns, Robert. **Poems**. London: John Hamilton, Ltd., n.d.

57. Bush, Robin. **Somerset: A Portrait in Colour**. Stanbridge: Dovecote Press, 1990.

58. Bussby, Frederick. **The History of Winchester Cathedral**. Southampton: Paul Cave Publication, Ltd., 1975.

59. Carlyle, Jane Welsh. **Jane Wesh Carlyle: A New Selection of Her Letters**. London: Victor Gollancz, 1950.

60. Carlyle, Jane Welsh. **New Letters and Memorials of Jane Welsh Carlyle**. London: The Bodley Head, 1903. 2 vols. Only vol 1 being here present.

61. Carlyle, Thomas. **Carlyle's Essay on Burns**. Boston: D.C. Health & Co., 1896.

62. Carlyle, Thomas. **Essay on Burns**. Boston: Allyn & Bacon Co., 1895.

63. Carroll, Lewis. **The Adventures of Alice in Wonderland & Through the Looking-Glass**. London: The Heirloom Press, 1958.

64. **Cassell's French-English English-French Dictionary**.

Ernest A. Baker, ed. New York: Funk & Wagnalls Co., n.d.

65. Catullus. **Poems**. Translated by C.H. Sisson. New York: The Orion Press, 1967.

66. Chestnut, Mary B. **A Diary of Dixie**. Boston: Houghton-Mifflin Co., 1949.

67. Chevalier, Denys. **Klee**. New York: Crown Publishers, 1979.

68. **A Christmas Cracker: Being a Commonplace Selection of John Julius Norwich**. Huntington: Hambledon Press, 1983.

68a. Chute, B.J. Greenwillow. New York: E.P. Dutton & Co., 1956.

69. Chute, Marchette. **Shakespeare of London**. New York: E.P. Dutton & Co., 1949.

70. Clucas, Philip. **Britain: An Aerial Close-Up**. London: Coombe Books, 1988.

71. **Colloquium: Helene Hanff**. Kaoru Haga, ed. Japan, 1986.

72. **The Complete Rhyming Dictionary and Poet's Craft Book**. Clement Wood, ed. Garden City: Garden City Books, 1936.

73. **Concise Dictionary of American History**. Thomas Cochran, ed. New York: Charles Scribner's Sons, 1962.

74. Conrad Barnaby III. **The Martini: An Illustrated History of an American Classic**. San Francisco: Chronicle Books, 1995.

75. Cook, Blanche W. **Eleanor Roosevelt**. New York: Penguin Books, 1993.

76. Cooper, Susan. **The Dark Is Rising**. New York: Aladdin Books, 1986.

77. Copland, Aaron. **What to Listen for in Music**. New York: New American Library, 1967.

78. Corrigan, Felicitas. **The Nun, the Infidel, and the Superman: The Remarkable Friendships of Dame Laurentia McLachlan with Sydney Cockerell, Bernard Shaw and Others**. Chicago: Chicago University Press, 1985.

79. Coward, Noel. **The Noel Coward Diaries**. Graham Payne, ed. Boston: Little, Brown & Co., 1982.

80. Coward, Noel. **Play Parade**. Garden City: Garden City Publishing Co., 1933.

81. Cunningham, E.V. **The Wabash Factor**. New York: Delacorte Press, 1986.

82. Daniel, Oliver. **Stokowski: A Counterpoint of View**. New York: Dodd, Mead & Co., 1982.

83. Davis, Adelle. **Let's Eat Right to Keep Fit**. New York: New American Library, 1970.

84. Davis, Adelle. **Let's Get Well**. New York: New American Library, 1965.

85. **Dear Miss Heber: An Eighteenth Century Correspondence**. Francis Bamford, ed. London: Constable, 1936.

86. Delafield, E.M. **Diary of a Provincial Lady**. London: Macmillan & Co., 1942.

87. Della Femina, Jerry. **From Those Wonderful Folks Who Gave You Pearl Harbor**. New York: Simon & Schuster, 1970.

88. Dickens, Charles. **Sketches by Boz**. London: Chapman & Hall, 1898. 2 vols. From Works.

89. Donne, John. **The Complete Poems of John Donne**. Roger Bennett, ed. Chicago: Packard & Co., 1942.

90. Donne, John. **The Complete Poetry and Selected Prose of John Donne and the Complete Poetry of William Blake**. New York: The Modern Library, 1946.

91. Donne, John. **Complete Poetry and Selected Prose of John Donne**. London: The Nonesuch Press, 1949.

92. Donne, John. **Devotions Upon Emergent Occasions**. John Sparrow, ed. Cambridge: The University Press, 1923.

93. Donne, John. **Donne's Sermons: Selected Passages**. Logan Pearsall Smith, ed. Oxford: Clarendon Press, 1942.

94. Donne, John. **Love Poems of John Donne: With Some Account of His Life by Izaak Walton**. London: The Nonesuch Prss, 1923. No. 191 Of 1250 cc.

95. Donne, John. **The Poems of John Donne**. Herbert Grierson,

ed. Oxford: The Clarendon Press, 1912.

96. Donne, John. **Poems of Love**. Kingsley Hart, ed. London: The Folio Society, 1958.

97. Donne, John. by J.D. with Elegies on the Author's Death. London: John

Marriot, 1650.

98. Donnelly, Liza. **Husbands and Wives**. New York: Ballantine Books, 1995.

99. Dos Passos, John. **The Head and Heart of Thomas Jefferson.** Garden City:

Doubleday & Co., 1954.

100. Dos Passos, John. **The Men Who Made the Nation**. Garden City: Doubleday & Co., 1957.

101. Du Maurier, Daphne. **Growing Pains: The Shaping of a Writer**. London: Victor Gollancz Ltd., 1977.

102. Duff, Charles. **The Lost Summer: The Heyday of the West End Theatre**. London: Heinemann, 1995.

103. Eagle, Dorothy. **The Oxford Literary Guide to the British Isles**. Oxford: The Clarendon Press, 1977.

104. **Eighteenth Century Essays**. Austin Dobson, ed. New York: D. Appleton & Co., 1889.

105. Ellis, Edward Robb. **A Nation in Torment: The Great American Depression, 1929 - 1939**. New York: Coward, McCann & Geohagen, 1970.

106. Emanuel, Nanette. **Creature Comforts: Poems**. n.p., n.d.

107. **The English Familiar Essay**. William Frank Bryan and Ronald Crane, eds. Boston: Ginn & Co., 1916.

108. Episcopal Church. **Liturgy and Ritual**. New York: The Church Pension Fund, 1945.

109. Evelyn, John. **The Diary of Evelyn John, esquire, F.R.S**. William Bray, ed. London: Simpkin, Marshall et al & Co., n.d.

110. Evelyn, John. **The Diary of Evelyn John esquire, F.R.S**. William Bray, ed. London: George Newnes Ltd., n.d.

111. **Familiar Quotations: A Collection of Passages, Phrases and Proverb**s. John Bartlett, ed. Boston: Little, Brown & Co., 1968.

112. Firkins, Oscar W. Two Passengers for Chelsea. London: Longmans, Green & Co., 1928.

113. Fitch, George Hamlin. **Comfort Found in Good Old Books**. San Francisco: Paul Elder & Co., 1911.

114. Fowler, H.W. **A Dictionary of Modern English Usage**. New York: Oxford
University Press, 1950.

115. Fowler, H.W. **The King's English**. Oxford: The Clarendon Press, 1970.

116. Freeman, Jane. **Jane Austen in Bath**. Alton: The Jan Austen Society, 1969.

117. Freud, Sigmund. **The Interpretation of Dreams**. Translated by James Strachey. London: George Allen & Unwin Co., 1954.

118. Friederich, Otto. **Before the Deluge: A Portrait of Berlin in the 1920's.** New York: Harper & Row, 1972.

119. Frost, Robert. **Selected Poems**. London: William Heinemann, 1923.

120. Garretson, John. **The School of Manners. Or Rules for Children's Behaviour.** London: The Oregon Press, Ltd., 1983. Facsimile reprint.

121. Gessner, Clark. **You're a Good Man Charlie Brown!** Greenwich: Fawcett Publications, 1970.

122. Gibbon, Edward. **The Decline and Fall of the Roman Empire**. London: Penguin Books, Ltd., n.d. 2 vol.

123. Gilbert, W.S. **The Savoy Operas.** London: Macmillan & Co., 1957, Volume 1 only is present.

124. Gleason, Clarence W. **A Greek Primer**. New York: American Book Co., 1931.

125. Golden, Harry. **Enjoy, Enjoy!** Cleveland: The World Publishing Co., 1958.

126. **The Golden Treasury with Additional Poems**. F.T. Palgrave,

ed. London: Collins" Cleartype Press, Ltd., n.d.

127. Gosse, Edmund. **Modern English Literature.** New York: D. Appleton & Co., 1928.

128. Grafton, Sue. **"G" Is for Gumshoe.** New York: Fawcett Crest, 1993.

129. Grafton, Sue. **"I"Is for Innocent.** New York: Fawcett Crest, 1993.

130. Grafton, Sue. **"K" Is for Killer.** New York: Fawcette Crest, 1993.

131. Grahame, Kenneth. **The Wind in the Willows.** Illustrated by Ernest Shepard. London:: Methuen & Co., Ltd., 1958.

132. Gray, Thomas. **The Poems of Gray and Collins.** London: George Newnes, 1905.

133. Greater New York Album: **One Hundred Selected Views.** Chicago: Rand, MaNally & Co., 1895.

134. **Gross, S. Cats** by Gross. New York: Ballantine Books, 1995.

135. Haga Kaoru. **American Literature** [Japanese title]. Japanese Publisher, 1992. Inscribed to Helene Hanff. Contains an essay entitled "Helene Hanff and Anglophilism."

136. Hall, Donald. **Remembering Poets: Reminiscences and Opinions.** New York: Harper & Rowe, 1978.

137. **Hamilton's Excursions Across the Atlantic Through America and Home Again within Two Hours!** No author. London, n.d.

138. Handel, George Frederick. **The Messiah: A Sacred Oratorio.** London: Novello & Co., Ltd., 1942.

139. Harris, Jed. **A Dance on the High Wire: Recollections of a Time and a Temperament.** New York: Crown Publishers, 1979.

140. Harvey, Sir Paul. **The Oxford Companion to English Literature.** Oxford: The Clarendon Press, 1983.

141. Hazlitt, William. **Characters of Shakespeare's Plays.** London: John Templeton, 1838.

142. Hazlitt, William. **Selected Essays of William Hazlitt, 1778-1830.** Geoffrey Keynes, ed. London: The Nonesuch Press, 1948.

143. Herriot, James. **All Creatures Great and Small**. New York: St. Martin's Press, 1972.

143a. Hibbert, Christopher. **The Tower of London**. New York: Newsweek, 1971.

144. Holmes, Oliver Wendell, Jr. **The Holmes Laski Letters, 1916 – 1935**. Cambridge: Harvard University Press, 1953. 2 vols.

145. Housman, A.E. **More Poems**. New York: Alfred A. Knopf, 1936.

146. Housman, A.E. **A Shropshire Lad**. Ludlow: Palmers Press, 1992.

147. Housman, A.E. **A Shropshire Lad**. New York: Hartsdale House, 1932.

148. Humphrey, Derek. **Final Exit: The Practicalities of Self-Deliverance and Assisted Suicide for the Dying**. Eugene: The Hemlock Society, 1991.

149. Hunt, Leigh. **The Autobiography of Leigh Hunt**. Oxford: Oxford University Press, 1936.

150. Hunt, Leigh. **Leigh Hunt As Poet and Essayist**. Charles Kent, ed. New York: Frederick Warne & Co., 1891.

151. Irving, Washington. **The Legend of Sleepy Hollow**. Drexill Hill: Bell Publishing Co., n.d. 152. Irving, Washington. The Sketch Book. New York: Literary Classics Co., 1945.

153. James, Henry. **New York Revisited**. New York: Franklin Square Press, 1994.

154. James, P.D. **A Mind to Murder**. New York: Warner Books, 1987.

155. [Japanese Bio-Bibliography of Helene Hanff.] 1980.

156. [Japanese Bio-Bibliography of Helene Hanff.] 1983.

157. Jefferson Reader: **A Treasury of Writings about Thomas Jefferson**. F. Rosenberger, ed. New York: E.P. Dutton & Co., 1953.

158. Jefferson, Thomas. **The Life and Selected Writings of Thomas Jefferson**. A. Kock and W. Peden, eds. New York: The Modern Library, 1944. 159. Jenkins, Elizabeth. **Elizabeth the Great**. New

York: Coward McCann, 1959.

160. Khan, Arona. **Wrap It Up!** London: Ward Lock, Ltd., 1987. Inscribed by the author to Helene Hanff.

161. Korelitz, Jean Hanff. **The Properties of Breath**. Newcastle Bloodaxe Books, 1988. Inscribed by the author to Helene Hanff.

162. Kraus, Barbara. **Calories and Carbohydrates**. New York: New American Library, 1979.

163. Lamb, Charles. **Everybody's Lamb**. A.C. Ward, ed. London: G. Bell and Sons, Ltd., 1933.

164. Lamb, Charles. **The Last Essays of Elia**. Philadelphia: Henry Altemus, 1899.

165. Landor, Walter Savage. **Imaginary Conversations.** London: Walter Scott Publishing Co., n.d.

166. Landor, Walter Savage. **The Works and Life of Walter Savage Landor**. London: Chapman & Hall, 1876. Volume 2 only is here present.

167. Lansbury, Coral. **Sweet Alice**. New York: E.P. Dutton & Co., 1989.

168. Lauder, Afterbeck. **Fraffley Well Spoken: How to Speak the Language of London's West End**. Sydney: Wolfe Publishing, 1968,

169. Lebrecht, Norman. **Hush! Handel's in a Passion: Tales of Bach**. London: Andre Deutsch, 1985.

170. Lee, Laurie. **Cider with Rosie**. London: The Hogarth Press, 1959.

171. Lewis, C.S. **The Joyful Christian: 127 Readings from C.S. Lewis.** New York: The Macmillan Co., 1977.

172. Lewis, C.S. **Mere Christianity**. New York: The Macmillan Co., 1975.

173. Lingeman, Richard R. **Don't You Know There's a War On?: The American Homefront, 1941 – 1945**. New York: G.P. Putnam's Sons, 1970.

174. Lipton, James. **An Exaltation of Larks: or The Venereal Game**. Grossman Publishers, 1968.

175. **Literary Walks of Britain.** Donald Veall, ed. Devizes: Select Editions, 1992.

176. **Love and Other Subjects: A Prejudiced Anthology.** Peter Gorb, ed. London: Privately Printed for Peter Gorb at the Lonsdale Press, 1995.

177. Lowell, James Russell. **Latest Literary Essays and Addresses.** Boston: Houghton-Mifflin & Co., 1892

178. **Lyrics from the Song-Books of the Elizabethan Age.** A.H. Bullen, ed. London: John C. Nimmo, 1889.

179. Lyttelton, George. **The Lyttelton – Hart-Davis Letters.** London: John Murray, 1978.

180. Macaulay, Thomas Babington. **Macaulay's Life of Samuel Johnson.** C.H. Hanson, ed. Boston: Ginn & Co., 1903.

181. Malone, Michael. **Handling Sin: A Novel.** Boston: Little, Brown & Co., 1986.

182. Martin, Brian. **John Henry Newman: His Life and Work.** London: Chatto & Windus, 1982.

183. McCrumb, Sharyn. **If I'd Killed Him when I Met Him.** New York: Ballantine Books, 1995.

184. Meyer, Edith M. **Enjoying Food on a Diabetic Diet.** New York: Doubleday & Co., 1974.

185. Millay, Edna St. Vincent. **The Harp-Weaver and Other Poems.** New York: Harper & Bros., 1923.

186. Millay, Edna St. Vincent. **The King's Henchman.** New York: Harper & Bros., 1927.

187. Millay, Edna St. Vincent. **Letters.** A.R. Macdougal, ed. New York: Harper & Bros., 1952.

188. Millay, Edna St. Vincent. **Poems.** London: Martin Secker, 1923.

189. Miller, Lewis. **Guide to Central Park.** Dearborn: Greenfield Village and Henry Ford Museum, 1977.

190. Milne, A.A. **Now We are Six.** New York: E.P. Dutton & Co., 1961.

191. Milne, A.A. **When We Were Very Young.** New York: E.P.

Dutton & Co., 1955.

192.   Milne, A.A. **Winnie-the-Pooh**. New York: E.P. Dutton & Co., 1954.

193.   Milton, John. **Complete Poetry and Selected Prose of John Milton**. New York: The Modern Library, n.d.

194.   Milton, John. **Minor Poems**. Boston: Alynn & Bacon, 1901.

195.   John Milton. **Selected Prose Writings of John Milton**. Ernest Meyers, ed. New York: New Amsterdam Book Co., 1904.

196.   Mitford, Nancy. **The Sun King**. New York: Harper & Row, 1966.

197.   **Modern American and Modern British Poetry**. Louis Untermeyer, ed. New York: Harcourt, Brace & Co., 1955.

198.   Monaghan, Frank. **This was New York: The Nations's Capitol in 1789**. Garden City: Doubleday, Doran & Co., 1943.

199.   Montaigne, Michel de. **Selected Essays**. Donald Frame, trans. and ed. New York: Walter J. Black, 1943.

200.   Montizambert, E. **Unnoticed London**. London: J.M. Dent & Sons, Ltd., 1925.

201.   Morley, Frank. **Literary Britain: A Reader's Guide to Its Writers and Landmarks**. New York: Harper & Row, 1980.

202.   Morris, James. **Farwell the Trumpets: An Imperial Retreat**. New York: Harcourt, Brace, Jovanovich, 1978.

203.   Moscow, Henry. **The Street Book: An Encyclopedia of Manyhattan's Street Names and Their Origins**. New York: Hagstrom Co., 1978.

204.   Musgrave, Clifford. **The Pictorial Story of Brighton, Past and Present**. London: Pitkins, Co., n.d.

205.   Nash, Ogden. **I Wouldn't Have Missed It**. Boston: Little, Brown & Co., 1982.

206.   Nash, Ogden. **A Penny Saved Is Impossible**. London: Andre Deutsch, 1982.

207.   **The New Columbia Encyclopedia**. W. Harris and J. Levey, eds. New York: Columbia University Press, 1975.

208. **The New Oxford Book of American Verse.** R. Elman, ed. New York: Oxford University Press.

209. **The New Oxford Book of English Verse**, 1250-1950. H. Gardner, ed. Oxford: Oxford University Press, 1989.

210. The New York Daily News. **Fifty Years in Pictures.** New York: Doubleday & Co., 1979.

211. New York: Verhalen van een Stad. **Amsterdam:** Meulenhoff, 1987. Contains an essay, "Tom Wolfe on Helene Hanff."

212. Newman, John Henry. **Apolgia Pro Vita Sua.** New York: Longmans, Green & Co., 1907.

213. Newman, John Henry. **A Newman Synthesis.** E. Pryzwara, ed. New York: Shed & Ward, 1945.

214. Newman, John Henry. **Tract Ninety: or, Remarks on Certain Passages in the Thirty-Nine Articles.** London: Constable & Co., Ltd., 1933.

215. Newman, John Henry. **University Subjects.** Boston: Houghton Mifflin Co., 1913.

216. O'Connor, Patrick. **Don't Look Back.** Wakefield: Moyer Bell, 1993.

217. O'Nolan, Brian. **The Best of Myles: A Selection from Cruisekeen Lawn.** O'Nolan, ed. London: Pan Books, 1975.

218. Omar Khayyam. **The Rubaiyat of Omar Khayyam Rendered into English Verse by Edward Fitgerald.** Philadelphia: Henry T. Coates & Co., 1898.

219. Omar Khayyam. **The Rubaiyat of Omar Khayyam Rendered into English Verse by Edward Fitzgerald.** New York: Grosset & Dunlap, 1971.

220. **The Oxford Book of English Verse**, 1250-1900. A.T. Quiller-Couch, ed. Oxford: The Clarendon Press, 1904.

221. **The Oxford Book of English Prose.** A.T. Quiller-Couch, The Clarendon Press, 1945.

222. **The Oxford Book of Essays.** John Gross, ed. Oxford: The Clarendon Press, 1991.

223. **The Oxford Dictionary of Quotations**. London: The Oxford University Press, 1964.

224. Pepys, Samuel. **The Diary of Samuel Pepys**, M.A., F.R.S.. Henry B. Wheatly, ed. London: G. Bell & Sons, 1926. Vols. 1-8 in 3.

225. Perry, Anne. **Traitor's Gate**. New York: Fawcett Crest, 1996.

226. **The Pilgrim's Way: A Little Scrip of Good Counsel for Travellers**. A.T. Quiller-Couch, ed. London: Seeley & Co., Ltd., 1906.

227. Pinter, Harold. **Poems and Pros, 1949-1977**. New York: Grove Press, 1978.

228. Piper, David. **The Companion Guide to London**. London: Collins, 1964. Inscribed to Helene Hanff by Pat Buckley.

229. Plato. **Apology:** Crito: Phaedo, etc. L.R. Loomis, ed., translated by B. Jowett. New York: Walter J. Black, 1942.

230. Plato. **The Philosophy of Plato**. New York: Carlton House, 1928.

231. Plomley, Roy. **Plomley's Pick of Desert Island Discs**. London: Weidenfield & Nicholson, 1982.

232. Plutarch. **Plutarch's Lives of Coriolanus**, Caesar, etc., in North's Translation. R.H. Carr, ed. Oxford: Clarendon Press, 1906.

233. **Poetry for Pleasure**. Selected by the Editors of Hallmark Cards, Inc. Garden City: Doubleday & Co., 1960.

234. **Poetry of the Restoration, 1653-1700**. V. de Sola Pinto, ed. London: William Heinemann, 1970.

235. **Poets' Corner: An Anthology**. E. Langford, ed. London: Chapmans, Ltd., 1992.

236. Pope-Hennessy, James. **Queen Mary, 1867 – 1953**. New York: Alfred A. Knopf, 1960.

237. Pritchett, V.S. **Lasting Impressions: Essays 1961–1987**. New York: Random House, 1990.

238. Quiller-Couch, Sir Arthur. **Adventures in Criticism**. New York: G.P. Putnam's Sons, 1925.

239. Quiller-Couch, Sir Arthur. **Charles Dickens and Other Victorians**. Cambridge: The University Press, 1925.

240. Quiller-Couch, Sir Arthur. **Exploring Shakespeare Country 100 Years Ago**. London: Thames and Hudson, 1985.

241. Quiller-Couch, Sir Arthur. **Green Bays**: Verses and Parodies by Q. London: Oxford University Press, 1930.

242. Quiller-Couch, Sir Arthur. **Memories & Opinions: An Unfinished Autobiography**. Cambridge: The University Press, 1945.

243. Quiller-Couch, Sir Arthur. **On the Art of Writing.** New York: G.P. Putnam's Sons, 1916.

244. Quiller-Couch, Sir Arthur. **On the Art of Reading.** New York: G.P. Putnam's Son's, 1920.

245. Quiller-Couch, Sir Arthur. **The Poet as Citizen.** New York: The Macmillan Co., 1935.

246. Quiller-Couch, Sir Arthur. **The Splendid Spur: Being Memoirs of the Adventures of Mr. John Marvel**. London: Thomas Nelson & Sons, Ltd., n.d.

247. Quiller-Couch, Sir Arthur. **Studies in Literature**: First Series. New York: G.P. Putnam's Sons, 1922.

248. Quiller-Couch, Sir Arthur. **Studies in Literature**: Second Series. New York: G.P. Putnam's Sons, 1926.

249. Quiller-Couch, Sir Arthur. **Studies in Literature**: Third Series. New York: G.P. Putnam's Sons, 1930.

250. Raleigh, Sir Walter. **Johnson on Shakespeare**. London: Oxford University Press, 1940.

251. Richards, G.C. **A Concise Dictionary to the Vulgate New Testament**. London: Samuel Bagster & Sons, Ltd., 1934.

252. Roberts, R. Ellis. **Reading for Pleasure and Other Essays**. London: Methuen & Co., Ltd., 1928.

253. Robertson, W. Graham. **Letters from Graham Robertson**. K. Preston, ed. London: Hamish Hamilton, 1953.

254. Robertson, W. Graham. **Time Was: Reminiscences of W. Graham Robertson**. London: Hamish Hamilton, 1945.

255. Roget, Peter. **Roget's International Thesaurus**. New York: Thomas Crowell Co., 1956.

256. **The Romance of Oxford: Guide and Souvenir**. Oxford: Chris Andrews Photographic Art, 1984.

257. Rostand, Edmond. **L'Aiglon**. C. Dane and R. Addinsell, eds. Garden City: Doubleday, Doran & Co., 1934.

258. Rowse, A.L. **The English Spirit: Essays in Literature and History**. London: Macmillan Co., 1966.

259. Rowse, A.L. Quiller-Couch: **A Portrait of Q**. London: Methuen & Co., 1988.

260. The Royal Pavilion Brighton. **Brighton**: Tourism Committee, 1982.

261. Saint-Simon, Louis de Rouvroy, duc de. **Memoires**. Translated and edited by F. Arkwright. London: Stanley Paul & Co., 1915-1918. 6 vols.

262. Sandburg, Carl. **Rainbows Are Made**. L. Hopkins, ed. New York: Harcourt, Brace, Jovanovich, 1982.

263. Schermerhorn, Gene. **Letters to Phil: Memories of a New York Boyhood**. New York: New York Bound, 1982. 264. A Seventeenth Century Anthology. A Meynell, ed. London: Blackie & Son, Ltd., n.d.

265. Shaffer, Peter. **Lettrice and Lovage: A Comedy.** New York: Harper & Row, 1990.

266. Shakespeare, William. **Complete Works of William Shakespeare**. Philadelphia: David McKay, n.d. 13 vols.

267. Shakespeare, William. **A Shakespearean Alphabet**. Stratford on Avon: Stratford Festival, 1985.

268. Shakespeare, William. **A Midsummer-Night's Dream**. London: William Heinemann, 1911.

269. Shakespeare, William. **The Sonnets of William Shakespeare**. L. Fox, ed. Norwich: Cotman House, n.d.

270. Shaw, George Bernard. **Bernard Shaw and Patrick Campbell: Their Correspondence**. Alan Dent, ed. London: Victor Gollancz, Ltd., 1952.

271. Shaw, George Bernard. **The Devil's Disciple**. New York:

Dodd, Mead & Co., 1941.

272.	Shaw, George Bernard. **Collected Letters, 1874-1897**. Dan Laurence, ed. New York: Dodd, Mead & Co., 1965.

273.	Shaw, George Bernard. **Dramatic Opinions and Essays with an Apology**. James Huneker, ed. New York: Brentano's, 1928.

274.	Shaw, George Bernard. **Major Barbara**. New York: Dodd, Mead & Co., 1930.

275.	Shaw, George Bernard. **Selected Plays with Prefaces**. New York: Dodd, Mead & Co., 1948. 4 volumes of which volumes 1 and 3 are here present.

276.	Shepard, Ernest H. **The House at Pooh Corner** by A.H. Milne. New York: E.P. Dutton & Co., 1961.

277.	Simpson, Loius. **Three on the Tower**: The Lives of Ezra Pound, T.D. Eliot and William Carlos Williams. New York: William Morrow & Co., 1975.

278.	Slayden, Ellen Maury. **Washington's Wife: A Journal**. New York: Harper & Row, 1963.

279.	Smith, Elsdon. **Dictionary of American Family Names**. New York: Harper & Bros., 1956.

280.	Soames, Sally. **Writers: Photographs.** London: Andre Deutsch, 1995. Contains a photograph of Helene Hanff.

281.	**The Social Register.** New York: Social Register Association, 1952.

282.	**The Standard Book of British and American Verse.** N. Braddy, ed. Garden City: Garden City Publishing, 1932.

283.	Stanislavski, Constantin. **An Actor Prepares**. New York: Theatre Arts, 1944.

284.	Stanislavski, Constantin. **Stanslavski Directs**. New York: Funk & Wagnalls, 1954.

285.	Sterne, Laurence. **The Life and Opinions of Tristram Shandy Gentleman**. New York: Macdonald & Co., 1950.

286. Stout, Rex. **The Doorbell Rang.** New York: Bantam Books, 1971.

287.	Strong, Roy. Elizabeth R. London: Secker & Warburg, 1971.

288. Suschitzky, Wolf. **Charing Cross Road in the Thirties**. London: Nishen Publishing, n.d.

289. Swift, Jonathan. **A Tale of a Tub and the Battle of the Books**. London: Hamish Hamilton, 1948.

290. Tebbel, John. **A Certain Club: One Hundred Years of the Players**, New York. New York: The Players, 1989.

291. Tennyson, Alfred Lord. **Poetical Works of Alfred Lord Tennyson**. London: Thomas Nelson & Sons, 1926.

292. Tennyson, Alfred Lord. **The Complete Works of Alfred Lord Tennyson, Poet Laureate**. New York: Frederick A. Stokes Co., 1891. 2 volumes of which volume 2 only is here present.

293. Terry, Ellen. **Ellen Terry and Bernard Shaw: A Correspondence**. London: Reinhardt & Evans, 1949.

294. Thirkell, Angela. **The Demon in the House**. Wakefield: Moyer Bell, 1996.

295. Thirkell, Angela. **Growing Up**. Wakefield: Moyer Bell, 1996.

296. **This Fabulous Century**. New York: Time-Life Books, 1969.

297. Thomas, Dylan. **Under Milkwood**. New York. New Directions, 1954.

298. Thomson, Virgil. **Selected Letters of Virgil Thomson**. T. Page and V. Weeks, eds. New York: Summit Books, 1988.

299. Thoreau, Henry David. **Walden and Other Writings**. Brooks Atkinson, ed. New York: The Modern Library, 1937.

300. Thurber, James. **The 13 Clocks**. New York: Donald I. Fine, 1990.

301. Toobin, Jerome. **Agitato: A Trek through the Musical Jungle.** New York: The Viking Press, 1975.

302. Toth, Susan Allen. **England as you Like It**. New York: Ballantine Books, 1995.

303. **The Treasury of Sacred Song**. F. Palgrave, ed. Oxford: The Clarendon Press, 1906.

304. Trollope, Anthony. **Barchester Towers**. New York: New American Library, 1984.

305.   Trollope, Anthony. **The Warden**. Oxford: The University Press, 1989.

306.   Tucker, George Herbert. **Jane Austen the Woman**. New York: St. Martin's Press, 1994.

307.   Twain, Mark. **The Adventures of Huckleberry Finn**. Toronto: Bantam Books, 1988.

308.   Vassiltchikov, Marie. **Berlin Diaries, 1940-1945**. New York: Alfred A. Knopf, 1987.

309.   Viorst, Judith. **People and Other Aggravations**. New York: New American Library, 1972.

310.   Viorst, Judith. **It's Hard to Be Hip Over Thirty and Other Tragedies of Married Life**. New York: World Publishing Co., 1970.

311.   Virgil. **Selections from Virgil's Ecologues and Georgics**. N. Gardinef, ed. Oxford: The Clarendon Press, 1928.

312.   Voltaire. **Candide**. New York: The Modern Library, n.d.

313.   Wagner, Richard. **The Ring of the Niebelung: A Trilogy with a Prelude**. London: William Heinemann, 1911.

314.   Walpole, Horace. **Selected Letters of Horace Walpole**. W.S. Lewis, ed. New Haven. Yale University Press, 1973.

315.   Walters, Minette. **The Dark Room**. London: Pan Books, 1996.

316.   Walton, Izaak. **The Compleat Angler or the Contemplative Man's Recreation**. Mount Vernon: The Peter Pauper Press, n.d. Inscribed to Helene Hanff by the publisher's son, Nick Beilen.

317.   Walton, Izaak. **The Compleat Anger or the Contemplative Man's Recreation**. London: J.M. Dent & Co., 1896.

318.   Warren, Charles. **Jacobin and Junto or Early American Politics as Viewed in the Diary of Dr. Nathaniel Ames, 1758 – 1822**. Cambridge: Harvard University Press, 1931.

319.   Watson, Francis. **The Year of the Wombat**: England, 1857. New York: Harper & Row, 1974.

320.   Waugh, Evelyn. **The Letters of Evelyn Waugh and Diane Cooper**. A. Cooper, ed. New York: Ticknor & Fields, 1992.

321. Webster, Jean. **Daddy Long-Legs.** New York: The Century Co., 1912.

322. Wentworth, Harold. **Dictionary of American Slang.** New York: Thomas Y. Crowell Co., 1960.

323. Wessely, J.E. Handy **Dictionary of the English and Spanish Languages.** Philadelphia: David McKay, n.d.

324. Wharton, Edith. **The Age of Innocence.** New York: Charles Scribner's Sons, 1970.

325. Wharton, Edith. **The Children.** New York: Collier Books, 1992.

326. Whitemore, Hugh. **The Best of Friends: Letters of Dame Laurentia McLachlan, Sydney Cockerel and George Bernard Shaw.** Oxford: Amber Lane Press, 1988.

327. Whitman, Walt. **Complete Poetry and Collected Prose. New** York: The Library of America, 1982.

328. Wilde, Oscar. **The Plays of Oscar Wilde.** New York: The Modern Library, n.d.

329. Williams, Niall. **O Come Ye Back to Ireland.** New York: Soho Publications, 1987.

330. Winter, William. **Shadows of the Stage.** New York: The Macmillan Co.,1893.

331. **The Woman's Hour Book.** W. Knowles and K. Evans, eds. London: Sidgwick & Jackson, 1981.

332. Woolf, Virginia. **The Common Reader:** First Series. London: The Hogarth Press, 1957.

333. Woolf, Virginia. **The Common Reader:** Second Series. London: The Hogarth Press, 1959.

334. Wright, R.W.M. **The City of Bath.** London: Pitkin Pictorials, Ltd., 1973.

Screenplays by Helene Hanff

Show	Episode
Hallmark Hall Of Fame	The Ordeal of Thomas Jefferson
Hallmark Hall Of Fame	The Lady in the Wings
Hallmark Hall Of Fame	Soldier's Bride
Hallmark Hall Of Fame	The Reluctant Redeemer
Hallmark Hall Of Fame	The Pirate and the Lawyer
Hallmark Hall Of Fame	No Man Is an Island
Matinee Theatre	The Carefree Tree
Matinee Theatre	The Riddle of Mary Murray
Matinee Theatre	Sweetheart, Wife or Mother
Matinee Theatre	She's the One With the Funny Face
Matinee Theatre	The Sport
Matinee Theatre	Emma
Matinee Theatre	Miss Morissa
Matinee Theatre	Pride and Prejudice
Matinee Theatre	Aesop and Rhodope
Matinee Theatre	The Heart's Desire
Matinee Theatre	Some Man Will Want You
The Adventures of Ellery Queen	Dead Secret
The Adventures of Ellery Queen	Rehearsal for Murder
The Adventures of Ellery Queen	Murder to Music
The Adventures of Ellery Queen	The High Executioner
The Adventures of Ellery Queen	The Adventure of the Ballet Murder
The Adventures of Ellery Queen	Dance of Death
The Adventures of Ellery Queen	Custom Made
The Adventures of Ellery Queen	Ready for Hanging

Other(11)

Show	Role	Episode
Hallmark Hall Of Fame	Teleplay	The Hands of Clara Schumann
Hallmark Hall Of Fame	Teleplay	Aimée de Rivery

Hallmark Hall Of Fame	Teleplay	Aesop and Rhodope
Hallmark Hall Of Fame	Teleplay	The Armour-Bearer
Hallmark Hall Of Fame	Teleplay	Petticoat Revolution
Hallmark Hall Of Fame	Teleplay	Patrick Henry
Matinee Theatre	Teleplay	Bachelor Father
Matinee Theatre	Teleplay	There's Always Juliet
Matinee Theatre	Teleplay	The Little Minister
Matinee Theatre	Teleplay	The Remarkable Mr. Jerome
Play for Today	Story	84 Charing Cross Road

Appendix

The following pages are a sampling of a parody of *84 Charing Cross Road* entitled, "84 Charlie Horse Road" by "Reginald Bloof." It was published in its entirety in Sick magazine in the late 1990s. The typescript was submitted to Moyer, Bell and promptly and, thankfully, rejected. Nonetheless, it is offered up here as an example of how far-reaching Helene's "little book" was and is.

Helene Hanff's books

84 Charlie Horse Road

1442 1/2 Crab Street
Hoboken, New Jersey
Dear FPD,

The books arrived and I'm quite pleased; the mustard stains came off with a squirt of Ajax and a little elbow grease. Of course, it was probably Grey Poupon, you fancy little stuffed shirt! I'm looking for the Imaginary Conversations (Vol 3, I think) you know the one between Jack Kennedy and Bill Clinton where Jack is talking about the Monroe Doctrine (Marilyn, that is) and how to sneak women into the Lincoln Bedroom and Bill is asking for permission to "comfort" Jacqueline. If you've got it, please send it over. I've enclosed $12.00 in food stamps. They should be good over there and I think it about equals 100 pounds (of Twinkies, that is). I 'm quite good at math, but I'll never figure out pence and pounds and crowns and all that other stupid stuff you euros call money!

SWAK
hh

PS: I hope Madam means over there what it means over here; I could use a good job!

Helene Hanff: *A Life*

84 Charlie Horse Road
Big Macks & Co. Used Books
84 Charlie Horse Road
Liverpool

Dear Mrs. Humpff:
We've come across a wonderful vinyl-bound copy of "Collected Letters to Penthouse Magazine, 1979." We're sending it along with an invoice together with a photo of all of us at 84 Charlie Horse Road with the hope that you might send us some of those wonderful American cigarettes you're chain-smoking (and maybe a little weed; very difficult to obtain over here since the War). I'm the gent on the far left with the goatee and the glass eye standing behind Miss Haversham in just the right position to gaze down her blouse. She can't type a letter in under an hour without at least 6 mistakes, but with those duckies, she's got more job security than a US Postal worker.
Adieu, mon ami

FPD

P.S. That S&H green stamp you used for postage didn't work. Her Majesty's Postal Service hit us for a quid. Kindly refrain from that practice in the future, fatso. F.

1442 1/2 Crab Street
Hoboken, New Jersey

Dear Ferdy,

I thought all you Brits were queer. What a relief to see one look and act the real man. Mildred, my good "friend" of 47 years asks if that's a bookmark in your pocket or are you just happy to have a copy of Dolly Parton's latest poster. I've sent over to you several gallon jugs of pigs' feet for Bastille Day. They gave them to us at the soup kitchen for Easter dinner and I'm a Moslem (with a Buddhist aunt, an Albanian Orthodox cousin, 3 atheist sisters and a Shinto half brother that was a Karnikazi pilot in WWII) and can't even look at that crap let alone eat it. Dig in podner. Have you found that May,1961 copy of TV Guide yet? The one with Jim Nabors in drag on the cover?

xxx
ooo
hh

1442 1/2 Crab Street
Hoboken, New Jersey

To ALL at Big Macks & Co:
EMERGENCY! !! Those pigs' feet I sent weren't fresh!!! 2 years past
the "Safe" date. Tomaine or tpomaine or something like that. Got a
call from my caseworker. Don't eat!!

Oops,
hh

P.S. I'm trying that Green Stamp trick again. I think it'll work this time.

Big Macks &Co.
Used Books
84 Charlie Horse Road
Liverpool

Dear Mrs. Humpff:
I work at Big Macks & Co and want to thank you for my share out ofthe pigs' feet you sent. I can't eat them myself, luv, but I've sent them off to mummsey at Heathbar-on-Snyde. Can't remember when she's seen so much pig in one place; at least not since the the Queen, Margaret and Fergie had lunch together, if you know what I mean dearie.

Please, please, for God's sake don't tell Ferdie I've written to you. He thinks you're all his and God knows what else I'll have to put up with if he finds out; I've about given up on running around the desk. I've even tried pasting a raisin to my upper lip to feign herpes. Nothing will stop him.

With cordial regards,
P. Honeypot Haversham (Divorced) Secretary

P.S. Please say nothing. I know you' ll understand. Ferdie says you're so sweet.

Helene Hanff: *A Life*

Big Macks & Co.
Used Books
84 Charlie Horse Road
Liverpool

Dear Helen:
We're all feeling the gloomy lot of late, what with the Queen still alive, discovering that Prince Andrew is a fairy and dear old Radames Flerd our cataloguer of 71 years passing on from food poisoning. He was so happy to receive my share out of the pigs' feet; at least he went out with a smile on that toothless face of his. His maiden aunt with whom he resided died that same night; fell right over in her plate with a thud and a woosh of gas, as they say. The old biddy didn't give him a moment's peace, bless her soul.

My wife Flora, an Irish lass (my third wife) sends you her best; she traded the photo of Englebert Humperdink you sent me for a Tom Jones glossy; she's all aflutter if you get my meaning.

We've come across that Polish-Swahili Dictionary you asked for and have sent it posthaste together with an invoice for 14 drachma. The signed Renee Richards is proving something of a task, but we'll keep at it. Just part of the Big Macks & Co. service.

Love and such,
Ferdie

123 Smarming Mews
Flat 4F
Liverpool

Dear Mrs. Humpff:

I am Ferdie' s's wife. Do ye understand, WIFE. We have 6 wee ones runnin' amok the house. All he talks about is Mrs. Humpff this and Mrs. Humpff that. Begora, if I ever get me hands on ye, every drunk in County Cork will na be able to save yer fat buttucks.

Flora
P.S. Please fergive me grarnmer.

Helene Hanff: *A Life*

1442 1/2 Crab Street
Hoboken, New Jersey

Dear Ferdie,

Just received the beautiful copy of "Donny Osmond in the Buff' that you sent. I love the feel of smooth glossy pages with the coffee and grease stains that some other previous owner has left behind. I turned to one of the pages where Donny is showing his cute derriere and someone, in bold black crayon wrote "Eat this!" and I shouted "Comrade!" You know Ferdie, I think you feel the same way ... about Donny, I mean. You're the only creep alive who understands me. Still breathin' you old SOB?

Love,
hh

APPENDIX 2

The following are copies of some pages of Helene Hanff's Probate Proceedings in the City of New York Probate Court.

Death Certificate

LAST WILL AND TESTAMENT

OF

HELENE HANFF

I, HELENE HANFF residing in the City, County and State of New York, do hereby make, publish and declare this instrument to be my Last Will and Testament, hereby revoking all Wills and Codicils by me at any time heretofore made.

FIRST: I authorize and empower my Co-Executors hereinafter named and any successor thereto, to pay, adjust and to compromise, in their sole discretion, any and all bills and claims asserted against my estate, and to pay same together with the cost of administering my estate, as soon as convenient after my demise.

SECOND: I have made known to my Executors my feelings about my funeral so that I direct that my Executors are to determine the nature of my funeral and I give them the absolute right to decide where I shall be buried.